FACTS ON ACTS
(of Apostles)

FACTS ON ACTS
(of Apostles)

by
Rev. Albert Joseph Mary Shamon

PUBLISHING COMPANY
P.O Box 42028 Santa Barbara, CA 93140-2028
(800) 647-9882 • (805) 957-4893 • Fax: (805) 957-1631

©1996 Queenship Publishing

Library of Congress Number # 96-69339

Published by:
    Queenship Publishing
    P.O. Box 42028
    Santa Barbara, CA 93140-2028
    (800) 647-9882 • (805) 957-4893 • Fax: (805) 957-1631

Printed in the United States of America

ISBN: 1-882972-65-1

CONTENTS

PREFACE

This little book is written for the average Catholic lay person. It is meant to open up the important book of Acts.

My hope is that readers will see how the Church grew after the Ascension of Our Lord; will see the action of the Holy Spirit in that growth; will discover how valid is the primacy of Peter, will begin to understand why Paul is the greatest missionary in the Church; and will glean some background to his Letters.

I have included the text of Acts, so that there will be no need to go to a Bible.

I hope this booklet will be used for personal meditation, in adult Bible study groups, and in high school CCD Bible classes.

Acts is the sequel to Luke's gospel. The Lucan gospel was probably written in Caesarea when Paul was imprisoned there between 58-60 A.D.; and the Acts while Paul was imprisoned in Rome between 61-63 A.D.

Albert Joseph Mary Shamon
Feast of St. Joseph the Worker
May 1, 1992

INTRODUCTION

Acts in general.
In one sense Acts is the most important book in the New Testament. For without it, we would know almost nothing of the early Church.

There are two ways of writing history: the way of the **annalist**, who takes events and records them as they happen, in strict chronological order; or the way of the **personalist**, who takes great personalities of history and vividly portrays events through them.

St. Luke in writing the Acts has used the personalist approach, for he focuses his story on the exploits and adventures of some of the great heroic figures of the early Church: Peter, Stephen, Philip, Barnabas, Paul and others.

The title.
Actually the title of the book in Greek is "Acts of Apostles," not "*The* Acts of *the* Apostles." There are no "the's" in the title. For Acts is not the story of all the apostles, but only of Peter and Paul. Most of the other apostles exercised their missionary activities beyond the boundaries of the Roman Empire. A fitting title could be "Acts of Apostolic Men."

The author.
Although the book itself doesn't say so, it has been held from earliest times that St. Luke wrote it. We don't know too much about Luke. There are only three references to him in the New Testament. From these we learn that Luke was a doctor (Col. 4:14), Paul's co-worker (Philemon 24) and his loyal friend during his last imprisonment (2 Tm.4:11). Very probably Luke was a Gentile, a Syrian from Antioch. In Colossians 4:11, St. Paul concludes a list of those who send greetings as "of the circumcision"; that is, Jews.

In verse 12, he begins a new list, the obvious inference is that these are not of the Jews, but Gentiles. Luke is in that list. So we have an interesting fact, namely, Luke is the only Gentile author in the New Testament.

When written.

The last sentence of Acts mentions that Paul "remained for two full years in his lodgings" (28:30). Paul was a prisoner in Rome for two years (61-63 A.D.) during which he wrote the Captivity Epistles: Colossians, Ephesians, Philemon and perhaps Philippians. Paul was set free in 63 A.D. because of lack of evidence.

So Acts was written during those two years of Paul's imprisonment. St. Luke says it was written after his gospel (Acts 1:1), which was probably written while Paul was a prisoner in Caesarea (58-60 A.D.).

Why written?

One reason why Luke wrote Acts was to provide Theophilus and others like him with the assurance that the teachings of the apostles were grounded in the teachings of Jesus; that the apostles had been chosen by Jesus and approved by Him to be witnesses of the resurrection.

Secondly, almost all the troubles for Christians so far had resulted from the animosity of the Jews. Luke hoped that the impressive and convincing story of Christianity thus far, written in fine literary Greek, would justify Christians against future Jewish calumny.

Also, Luke wanted to win Romans in high places to Christianity. So he made it clear that it was the Jews, not the Romans, who had first persecuted Christians. He has no criticism for Romans. Rather he shows that Roman magistrates were most courteous and fair to Christians and found nothing reprehensible in them. He points out that the governor of Cyprus, Sergius Paulus, became a Christian (Acts 13:12); that the magistrates of Philippi apologized to Paul and Silas for having had them scourged (Acts 18:14); and that Festus declared Paul innocent (Acts 25); that three times Romans saved Paul's life (Acts 21:32; 23:10; 27:43).

(The suggestion has been made that Acts was the brief prepared by Luke for Paul's defense when he stood trial before Caesar.)

Thirdly, Luke wrote Acts to show that Christianity is a Universal Religion, ordained for all peoples and for all nations. Such a concept was novel to and hard for a Jew to grasp. The Jews had only the Old Testament. In it, God had chosen them as His people. God had made a covenant with them. God had sent the Messiah to them. So it is easy to see how they could have developed a religious exclusivism, and could feel that God was concerned only with them. Hence Judaism was never a missionary religion.

Luke proves that it was God Himself who broke through the boundaries set up by His people. Stephen, filled with the Spirit, dies for universalism; the Holy Spirit sends Philip to Samaria and to the Ethiopian eunuch of the Candace; the same Holy Spirit impels Peter to receive Cornelius into the Church: at Antioch the followers of Jesus are called Christians; and there at Antioch, the Holy Spirit sets Paul and Barnabas apart to evangelize the Gentiles.

In other words, Luke shows that Christianity is a missionary religion. It took many, many interventions of the Holy Spirit to make the apostles conscious of this fact.

To reveal this missionary expansion, Luke used the device of the TRAVELOGUE: he describes (1) actual journeys by foot and by boat, and (2) the mental journeys, the changes that took place in religious ideas.

The foot journey. Luke's gospel is a travelogue from Galilee to Jerusalem; the central figure is Christ. He goes up to Jerusalem, the center of the ancient religion, and by the Paschal mystery, His death, resurrection, and ascension, founds the religion that perfects Judaism. The gospel ends with Jesus' ascension into heaven.

The Acts is a travelogue from Jerusalem to Rome. The central figure is Paul. He goes up to Jerusalem; but to escape the Sanhedrin, he appeals to Caesar and thus is sent to Rome, the center of the world.

The mental journey. The gospel begins in the Temple in Jerusalem and ends at Bethany, outside Jerusalem. The events narrated in-between point out dramatically that a complete transformation has taken place in the concept of divine cult and religion.

Acts begins with the Kingdom of God and ends with it. But the events narrated in-between also show dramatically that a complete evolution has taken place in the concept of the Kingdom of

God: no longer is it seen as exclusively Jewish and a political kingdom, but as a universal and spiritual kingdom, leading all men to eternal life. Acts records the journey from Judaism to Christianity, from the Mosaic Law to grace, from the Kingdom of God to the Church of God.

Faith without good works is dead; therefore, it was fitting that Luke's gospel, a book of Facts, be followed by Luke's travelogue, a book of Acts.

Acts 1:1-26
Revised New Testament

I. The Preparation for The Christian Mission

1. The Promise of the Spirit [1] In the first book, Theophilus, I dealt with all that Jesus did and taught [2] until the day he was taken up, after giving instructions through the Holy Spirit to the apostles whom he had chosen. [3] He presented himself alive to them by many proofs after he had suffered, appearing to them during forty days and speaking about the kingdom of God. [4] While meeting with them, he injoined them not to depart from Jerusalem, but to wait for "the promise of the Father about which you have heard me speak; [5] for John baptized with water, but in a few days you will be baptized with the Holy Spirit."

The Ascension of Jesus [6] When they had gathered together they asked him, "Lord, are you at this time going to restore the kingdom to Israel?" [7] He answered them, "It is not for you to know the times or seasons that the Father has established by his own authority. [8] But you will receive power when the Holy Spirit comes upon you, and you will be my witnesses in Jerusalem, throughout Judea and Samaria, and to the ends of the earth." [9] When he had said this, as they were looking on, he was lifted up, and a cloud took him from their sight. [10] While they were looking intently at the sky as he was going, suddenly two men dressed in white garments stood beside them. [11] They said, "Men of Galilee, why are you standing there looking at the sky? This Jesus who has been taken up from you into heaven will return in the same way as you have seen him going into heaven." [12] Then they returned to Jerusalem from the mount called Olivet, which is near Jerusalem, a sabbath day's journey away.

The First Community in Jerusalem [13] When they entered the city they went to the upper room where they were staying, Peter and John and James and Andrew, Philip and Thomas, Bartholomew and Matthew, James son of

Alphaeus, Simon the Zealot, and Judas son of James. [14] All these devoted themselves with one accord to prayer, together with some women, and Mary the mother of Jesus, and his brothers.

The Choice of Judas's Successor [15] During those days Peter stood up in the midst of the brothers (there was a group of about one hundred and twenty persons in the one place). He said, [16] "My brothers, the scripture had to be fulfilled which the Holy Spirit spoke beforehand through the mouth of David, concerning Judas, who was the guide for those who arrested Jesus. [17] He was numbered among us and was *allotted* a share in this ministry. [18] [He bought a parcel of land with the wages of his iniquity, and falling headlong, he burst open in the middle, and all his insides spilled out. [19] This became known to everyone who lived in Jerusalem, so that the parcel of land was called in their language 'Akeldama.' that is, Field of Blood.] [20] For it is written in the Book of Psalms: 'Let his encampment become desolate, and may no one dwell in it.' And 'May another take his office.'

[21] Therefore, it is necessary that one of the men who accompanied us the whole time the Lord Jesus came and went among us, [22] beginning from the baptism of John until the day on which he was taken up from us, became with us a witness to his resurrection." [23] So they proposed two, Joseph called Barsabbas, who was also known as Justus, and Matthais. [24] Then they prayed, "You, Lord, who know the hearts of all, show which one of these two you have chosen [25] to take the place in this apostolic ministry from which Judas turned away to go to his own place." [26] Then they gave lots to them, and the lot fell upon Matthias, and he was counted with the eleven apostles.

CHAPTER 1

The Promise of the Spirit

The Promise of the Spirit (1:1-5). St. Luke begins Acts this way: "In the first book, Theophilus..." The first book was his gospel, written between 58-60 A.D. Acts was written to the same person, Theophilus (God-lover). He may have been a Christian leader, wealthy enough to have Luke's Gospel and Acts published.

In his gospel Luke dealt with all that Jesus had done and taught. So often we are long on talk and short on deeds. Actions speak louder than words. Jesus practiced what He preached long before He taught. For instance, He lived a hidden life for 30 years: 10 years of hiddenness for every year of public ministry. Acts tells what Jesus continues to do and to teach in His Church through the Holy Spirit.

Luke's gospel ends with the ascension of Our Lord. The time from the resurrection of Jesus (April 9, 30 A.D.) to His ascension (May 19, 30 A.D.) was considered very sacred time by Luke; hence he used the sacred number forty (Dt. 8:2). In those forty days, Jesus proved the reality of His resurrection and instructed His disciples regarding the kingdom of God. He finally left them with the command that they were to wait in Jerusalem for the promise of the Father: baptism with the Spirit. Jesus came into the world to save sinners; He left it to save sinners by sending His Holy Spirit upon His Church.

The Ascension of Jesus (1:6-12). When Jesus and His disciples had gathered together on Mt. Olivet just before His Ascension, the apostles asked Jesus when He was going to restore the kingdom to Israel. Their question shows that they were still thinking of a political kingdom. When He had not restored it in His

3

public ministry, they wondered if He was going to restore it in the period of the Church.

In (Acts 2:3) God showed that His promise about the kingdom was about the coming of the Holy Spirit, not some earthly kingdom. So Jesus told them not to waste time on something unknown; rather He urged them to focus on the power of the Spirit and to use this power to give witness to Himself to the ends of the earth.

Christ had done the lion's share in regard to our salvation: He had laid the foundation of redemption by His Passion, death and resurrection. But He expects us to do our part: to erect the superstructure on the foundation. At Cana Jesus asked for water; at the miracle of loaves He used five loaves and two fish; etc. In other words, Jesus always solicited what others had or could do for working His miracles. So He expects us to do what we can do; namely, to become WITNESSES of His resurrection, like the apostles.

A witness is somebody who can say, "I know this is true, because I have seen and heard what I am telling you." A witness in court cannot testify by hearsay; the best witness is an eyewitness. Thus Jesus presented Himself alive to the apostles for 40 days so that their witnessing to His resurrection would be firsthand, from personal experiences. They could say, "I saw all this with my own eyes."

A witness is one who testifies not only by word, but especially by deeds. When Stanley discovered Livingston in Central Africa and had spent some time with him, he said, "Had I been there longer, I would have been compelled to become a Christian. He never spoke to me about it at all—but the witness of his life was irresistible."

The Greek word for witness is "martyr." A witness is one who is so certain of the truth of his testimony that he would be ready to lay down his life for it. Most of the heroes of Acts did just that.

Likewise, if we too are to be witnesses of our faith, we must have firsthand experience of Christ. To get this experience, we need to listen to His words in Scriptures each day, frequent the sacraments, especially the Holy Eucharist and Penance, and pray daily.

When Jesus had commanded the apostles to evangelize the world, the pagan world was ripe for the gospel. A mistake we sometimes make in discussing Christianity and other religions is to try to prove Christianity is true and all the other religions are false. That is not the proper approach.

Man, you see, is naturally religious. Religions have existed since the existence of man. They served a purpose: they answered man's basic needs and desires at that particular time in history. But unaided by divine revelation, man's religions were mythologies—inadequate, because false. In time, the inadequacies of his myths became apparent, and then man would seek elsewhere for a religion that would answer the desires of his heart. At the time of Acts, a great void existed in the religions of the day. Man was ready for a religion based on divine revelation, for theology, not mythology. Jesus' religion had come at the opportune time in history. Man was ready for the gospel.

When C.S. Lewis was seeking religion, he wrote: "The question was no longer to find the one simply true religion among a thousand religions simply false. It was rather, where has religion reached its true maturity? Where, if anywhere, have the hints of all paganism been fulfilled?"

"Paganism had been only the childhood of religion, or only a prophetic dream. Where was the thing full grown? Or where was the awakening?" (*Surprised by Joy,* pp. 187-88).

Thus Vatican II pointed out: "Men look to the various religions for answers to those profound mysteries of the human condition..." (Decl. on the Relationship of the Church to Non-Christian Religions, #1).

So, it is not a question of Christianity being true and the other religions false. No, it is simply a question that Christianity is the fullness of all religions; it is the fullness of truth, satisfying all the aspirations of the human heart. Hence its missionary character: Christianity has everything man wants and has been seeking. So Vatican II could state: "The Church has been divinely sent to all nations that she might be 'the universal sacrament of salvation'" (Decree on the Missionary Activity of the Church. #1).

After having commissioned the apostles to be witnesses of His resurrection to the ends of the earth, Jesus was lifted up, and a cloud took Him from their sight.

The ascension of Jesus was a disappearance, not a departure. He is still very much with us, at Mass. When He walked the earth, He accepted all the limitations of His humanity. That was His humility. So, He could be in only one place and space at a time. But after His ascension, He can be everywhere.

Take a lamp. Set it on the floor of a room. The bodies of persons around it will intercept its light, so that it cannot shine beyond them, to the remote corners of the room. But hoist the lamp to the ceiling, and it will shine to all in the house. So when Jesus was on earth, His presence was, as it were, localized. But lifted up to heaven, His presence is universalized—He is everywhere.

As the apostles witnessed the ascension, two men appeared; probably Moses and Elijah, the two who were with Jesus at His transfiguration. They announced that this Jesus would come again the same way He left, namely, in the sky. They didn't say when. The early Christians at first thought it would be soon—or so they hoped. But after this announcement, they all returned to Jerusalem from the Mount of Olives, to await, not the coming of Jesus again, but the coming of His Holy Spirit.

In 380 A.D. a round structure was built encircling the Rock of Ascension which is said to contain Christ's footprint. When it was destroyed, the Crusaders erected a polygonal chapel open to the sky. This chapel was enclosed by an octagonal wall. In 1187 the Moslems covered the chapel with a dome, which was the main inspiration for the Dome of the Rock Mosque, located on the site of Solomon's temple in Jerusalem.

The First Community in Jerusalem (1:13-14). When the apostles returned to the city, they went to the upper room where they were staying. The Upper Room was probably the room where Our Lord celebrated the Eucharist (the Cenacle).

Generally, in Jewish homes in Jerusalem, there was a second floor with a spacious room reserved for guests, especially for the feasts of Passover and Pentecost. This upper room was a kind of domestic chapel. The family assembled there to read the Law and to celebrate religious festivals. When Peter wanted to pray at Joppa, he went up to the roof terrace (Acts 10:9). Paul celebrated the breaking of bread in an upper room at Troas. On that occasion Eutyches fell from the window and Paul restored him to life. (Acts 10:4-12).

The upper room, where the apostles stayed at day and went to separate lodgings at night, was probably owned by Mary, the mother of John Mark, the evangelist.

The Choice of Judas' Successor (1:15-26). "During those days," that is the ten days between the Ascension and Pentecost, "Peter stood up in the midst of the brothers"—a group of 120.

When the apostles met in the Upper Room after the Ascension, they were aware they formed a distinct community. Hence Luke mentions the number of persons as being about 120—the number sufficient in ancient Jewish law to form a distinct community, like their Jewish Sanhedrin.

Following the pattern of the Sanhedrin, the apostles named Peter as their head. Then the core group, the apostles, are listed. They are listed in three groups of four, each group of four is headed, as in the gospels, by the same persons, namely, Peter, Philip, and James.

The apostles were persons of such diverse character and temperament, that humanly speaking one would have thought they could never have worked together. There was Matthew, once a collaborator with Rome. There was Simon called the "Zealot," either because of his violent opposition to Rome, or because of his zeal for Christ. Yet Jesus brought these opposites together in harmony—an indication that only He can bring unity to the world, which is a society of so many different personalities. He alone is our hope, who can make of all mankind one family.

"All these devoted themselves with one accord to prayer, together with some women, and Mary the mother of Jesus, and his brothers."

The church prayed. It prayed for nine days, the first novena. As repeated strokes of the brush are necessary for the painting or many strokes with hammer and chisel for the sculpture, so constancy in prayer is necessary for effective prayer. In Acts, there is a definite link between prayer and the coming of the Spirit, as between clouds and rain. The Greek word for "noise," used to describe the coming of the Spirit, is *echos*, as if to say the coming of the Spirit is the echo of prayer.

St. Luke makes special mention of Mary's being there. For she was the one who kept them all together and gave them perseverance. Mother of faith, she became mother of the Church. The Holy Spirit came upon Mary at the Annunciation to give her the grace to love Jesus as her child; on Pentecost the Holy Spirit came upon her to give her the grace to love all of us as her children. A love comparable to her love for Jesus was given to her for us on Pentecost.

The brothers of the Lord are simply his relatives. There was no word in Hebrew or Aramaic for cousin, so Old Testament writers used the word AH, brother, to describe different degrees of kindred. Nephews and cousins were called "brothers." Salome, the mother of James and John, was perhaps a cousin to Mary. Alphaeus, the father of Joses, Simon, James, Jude, was the brother of St. Joseph.

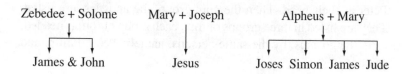

To have a Sanhedrin, the election of a successor to Judas was imperative. It is also possible that the apostles thought the Parousia was imminent and so they wanted the twelve thrones filled to be occupied by them in the final judgment of Israel (Mt. 19:28).

Jesus chose Twelve (Lk. 6:13). He did this to replace the Jewish leaders who had rejected Him. The old Israel had sprung from the 12 sons of Jacob; the twelve apostles were divinely appointed as the leaders of the new Israel.

In selecting a successor, it was Peter who presided. His reference to the Scriptures as the word of God showed he believed in its inspiration. He recalled Judas' part in the arrest of Jesus: "the guide for those who arrested Jesus."

Then in a kind of parenthesis (verse 18-19), information is given as to how Judas died. No one knows exactly how. Matthew describes his death in terms of the traitor Ahithophel, who betrayed David and then hanged himself (2 Sam. 17:23). Luke says Judas purchased a piece of land with the betrayal money, had a great fall there, and burst open in the middle. So people called the land a "Field of Blood" (Akeldama, in the Aramaic).

Peter laid down the conditions that needed to be observed in choosing Judas' successor. Since an apostle was to give witness to the resurrection of Jesus and His teaching, it was necessary that the one chosen be with Jesus from His baptism to His resurrection. Only two of the disciples appeared to qualify.

It is significant that the one called "Justus" was not selected. Man sees the outside; God sees the heart. Matthias was chosen.

It is to be noted well that the apostles chose a successor to Judas from two men not even mentioned in the gospels. They were nobodies. We know absolutely nothing about Matthias. And yet the Mother of God was there.

Mary was not chosen, because the apostles knew that the ordination of women was contrary to the will of Christ.

In the first centuries when Gnostics tried to ordain women, the Fathers of the Church condemned it. The reason given was that they must remain faithful to the type of ordained ministry willed by Christ and carefully maintained by the apostles.[1]

---

[1] The Sacred Congregation for the Doctrine of the Faith wrote: "' Sacramental signs,' says St. Thomas, 'represent what they signify by natural resemblance.' The same natural resemblance is required for persons as for things: when Christ's role in the Eucharist is to be expressed sacramentally, there would not be this 'natural resemblance' which must exist between Christ and his minister in the role of Christ were not taken by a man: in such a case it would be difficult to see in the minister the image of Christ. For Christ himself was and remains a man" (Inter Insigniores, 10/15/76, p. 12).

Equality does not mean identity! Nor does identity of function confer equality. Distinction of roles implies neither inferiority nor superiority. The greatest in the kingdom of heaven are not the ministers, but the saints.

Facts on Acts

Acts **2: 1-45**

2 [1] When the time for Pentecost was fulfilled, they were all in one place together. [2] And suddenly there came from the sky a noise like a strong driving wind, and it filled the entire house in which they were. [3] Then there appeared to them tongues of fire, which *parted and came* to rest on each one of them. [4] And they were all filled with the Holy Spirit and began to speak in different tongues, as the Spirit enabled them to proclaim.

[5] Now there were devout Jews from every nation under heaven staying in Jerusalem. [6] At this sound, they gathered in a large crowd, but they were confused because each one heard them speaking in his own language. [7] They were astounded, and in amazement they asked, "Are not all these people who are speaking Galileans? [8] Then how does each of us hear them in his own native language? [9] We are Parthians, Medes, and Elamites, inhabitants of Mesopotamia, Judea and Cappadocia, Pontus and Asia, [10] Phrygia and Pamphylia, Egypt and the districts of Libya near Cyrene, as well as travelers from Rome, [11] both Jews and converts to Judaism, Cretans and Arabs, yet we hear them speaking in our own tongues of the mighty acts of God." [12] They were all astounded and bewildered, and said to one another, "What does this mean?" [13] But others said, scoffing, "They have had too much new wine."

II. The Mission in Jerusalem

Peter's Speech at Pentecost [14] Then Peter stood up with the Eleven, raised his voice, and proclaimed to them, "You who are Jews, indeed all of you staying in Jerusalem. Let this be known to you, and listen to my words. [15] These people are not drunk, as you suppose, for it is only nine o'clock in the morning. [16] No, this is what was spoken through the prophet Joel:

[17] 'It will come to pass in the last days,' God says,
> 'that I will pour out a portion of my spirit
> upon all flesh.
Your sons and your daughters shall
> prophesy,
your young men shall see visions,
your old men shall dream dreams.
[18] Indeed, upon my servants and my handmaids
> I will pour out a portion of my spirit in
> those days, and they shall prophesy.
[19] And I will work wonders in the heavens above
> and signs on the earth below:
> blood, fire, and a cloud of smoke.
[20] The sun shall be turned to darkness,
> and the moon to blood,
> before the coming of the great and splendid day
> of the Lord,
[21] and it shall be that everyone shall be saved who calls
> on the name of the Lord.'

[22] You who are Israelites, hear these words. Jesus the Nazorean was a man commended to you by God with mighty deeds, wonders, and signs, which God worked through him in your midst, as you yourselves know. [23] This man, delivered up by the set plan and foreknowledge of God, you killed, using lawless men to crucify him. [24] But God raised him up, releasing him from the throes of death, because it was impossible for him to be held by it. [25] For David says of him:

'I saw the Lord ever before me,
> with him at my right hand I shall not be
> disturbed.
[26] Therefore my heart has been glad and my tongue has
> exulted;
my flesh too, will dwell in hope,
[27] *because you will not abandon my soul to the nether*
> *world,*

*nor will you suffer your holy one to see
    corruption.*
28 You have made known to me the paths of life;
    you will fill me with joy in your presence.'

29 My brothers, one can confidently say to you about
the patriarch David that he died and was buried, and his
tomb is in our midst to this day. 30 But since he was a *prophet*
and *knew that God had sworn an oath to him* that he would
set one of his descendants upon his throne, 31 he foresaw
and spoke of the *resurrection of the Messiah,* that neither
was he abandoned to the netherworld nor did his flesh see
corruption. 32 *God raised this Jesus; of this we are all witnesses.* 33 Exalted at the right hand of God, he received the
promise of the Holy Spirit from the Father and poured it
forth, as you [both] see and hear. 34 For David did not go up
into heaven, but he himself said:

    'The Lord said to my Lord,
      "Sit at my right hand
    35 until I make your enemies your footstool."'

36 Therefore let the whole house of Israel know for certain
that God has made him both Lord and Messiah, this Jesus
whom you crucified."
37 Now when they heard this, they were cut to the heart, and
they asked Peter and the other apostles, "What are we to do,
my brothers?" 38 Peter [said] to them, *"Repent and be baptized, every one of you, in the name of Jesus Christ for the
forgiveness of your sins; and you will receive the gift of the
Holy Spirit.* 39 For the promise is made to you and to your
children and to all those far off, whomever the Lord our God
will call." 40 He testified with many other arguments, and
was exhorting them, *"Save yourselves* from this corrupt generation." 41 Those who accepted his message were baptized,
and about three thousand persons were added that day.
Communal Life 42 They devoted themselves to the teaching of the apostles and to the communal life, to the breaking

of the bread and to the prayers. [43] Awe came upon everyone, and many wonders and signs were done through the apostles. [44] All who believed were together and had all things in common; [45] they would sell their property and possessions and divide them among all according to need.

CHAPTER 2

Pentecost and Peter's Discourse

Christ's public life began with the coming of the Spirit (28 A.D.); the Church's public ministry began with the coming of the Spirit (30 A.D.).

Pentecost (2:1-13). Pentecost means "the fiftieth" day. Originally, it was a thanksgiving feast for the spring harvest (Dt. 16:9-12). On the fiftieth day after Passover, thanks were given to God by offering Him the first fruits of the harvest. Later on, Pentecost became related to the giving of the Law on Mt. Sinai, fifty days after the Exodus.

The Jewish Pentecost, commemorating the giving of the Law on Mt. Sinai, foreshadowed the Christian Pentecost, the giving of the Holy Spirit in the Cenacle, fifty days after Passover (May 29, 30 A.D.). The wind and the fire at the Christian Pentecost recalled the wind and the fire of Sinai, Exodus 19:16-19.

The coming of the Holy Spirit transformed the community into something different from what the disciples had anticipated. They expected the baptism with the Spirit to usher in the Parousia and restore the political kingdom of Israel. So Luke takes great pains to describe the revolutionary character of the event.

First, the "NOISE like a strong driving WIND" was a sign of the new action of God in Salvation History. The noise was meant to awaken them; the wind, to move them.

A church organ needs wind to be played. So do the "wind" instruments in a symphony. Without wind, the organ is mute, and musical instruments soundless. With wind, there can be sound of great beauty. Likewise, without the Spirit, man is mute, his life sterile. With the Spirit, beauty enters his life and God is glorified.

Secondly, there were "TONGUES as of FIRE, which parted and came to rest on each one of them." The tongue is the instrument of speech. The Spirit would enable them to preach with fiery tongues; tongues that would save men from the fire of God's judgment.

Thirdly, "they began to speak in different tongues." The gift of tongues may be **unintelligible**—that is, praying to God and praising Him without words or without understanding. This is ecstatic prayer. In Corinth such praying sounded like incoherent babbling (1 Cor. 14:2,9,14). The fact that some of the people thought the apostles were drunk (Acts 2:12-15) seems to indicate that their speaking in tongues was ecstatic prayer.

Or the gift of tongues could be **intelligible,** not to the speakers, but to the hearers. We call this the gift of interpretation of tongues. In this way the hearers could share in the outpouring of the Spirit. In verses 6-11, Luke describes the gift of interpretation as speaking in foreign tongues, to signify the *worldwide mission of the Church.*

The Pentecost gift of tongues also symbolized the reversal of punishment at the Tower of Babel (Gn. 11:1-9). God is love, and love is unitive. The devil is hate, and hate and sin are divisive. Babel divided mankind; but the Spirit given at Pentecost would unite all mankind.

"They were all filled with the Holy Spirit"—not some, but all; not half-filled, but filled, not with spirits, but with the Spirit.

The result was they preached boldly and with understanding; unity was brought to the community, together with peace and joy.

An automobile needs gasoline; a locomotive needs steam. Without gas or steam neither vehicle would go. If a car or locomotive is stalled because one is out of gas and the other out of steam, the solution is not to put in new sparkplugs or to change the smokestack. All that is needed is gas and steam.

So with the problems of the world. People say, "This is what is needed." Politicians offer plans and projects. Yet nothing will help the world unless the Holy Spirit comes. He is the great need of the world. He alone can give it the gas and steam it needs.

In Jerusalem for Pentecost "there were devout Jews from every nation under heaven." Pentecost generally drew more people than Passover, for the season was better for traveling.

St. Luke lists 15 countries. Jews were dispersed over the then known world three times in their history.

Shalmaneser in 721 B.C. led ten of the tribes of Israel into the Assyrian Captivity—into Parthia, Media and Elam.

In 606 B.C. Nebuchadnezzar led the remaining tribes (Juda and Benjamin) into the Baylonian Captivity. Hence Mesopotamia, Judea and Cappadicia, Pontus and Asia, Phrygia and Pamphylia.

Finally, Ptolemy Lagus, one of the generals of Alexander the Great, in 329 encouraged Jews to settle in Alexandria, by granting them many privileges and high positions. Hence Egypt and Libya.

Lastly, Romans, Cretans and Arabs. The fact that great places like Syria, Achaia, Macedonia, Cyprus are missing shows that Luke was a good historian—he gave only the facts.

Peter's Speech at Pentecost (2:14-41). In Acts there are six discourses on the resurrection of Jesus: five are given by Peter, one by Paul. These discourses are called the *kerygma,* the proclamation (1 Cor. 15:11).

Just suppose you had been one of the twelve apostles, and you had been told to go teach all nations. What would you teach?

What could you teach? You had had no formal courses in theology. All you could talk about would be the one person you had known for three years, Jesus Christ. And what would you say about Him? Well, you would talk about the thing in His life that most struck you; namely, His passion, death, resurrection and ascension into heaven (the Paschal Mystery). What you would emphasize would be His resurrection from the dead, for this convinced you that Jesus was more than a man—that He was God! This was the Kerygma, the proclamation preached by Peter and Paul.

Peter was the first to proclaim the Kerygma after the coming of the Holy Spirit. He stood up and raised his voice: it must have been a booming voice—the voice of a fisherman, shouting to be heard above the waves. His discourse is divided into three parts.

Part 1 (2:14-21). The first thing Peter did was to defend the other apostles. "These people are not drunk," he thundered. "It is only 9:00 A.M." Jews fasted until 10:00 A.M. In the Old Testa-

17

ment, the Spirit's coming upon someone was often overwhelming and caused quite different or unusual behavior (cp. Saul's in 1 Sam 10:5-13).

Peter then proceeded to explain that the apostles' behavior was the fulfillment of Joel's prophecy. Joel prophesied (c. 400 B.C.) that "afterward, I will pour out my spirit upon all mankind" (3:1). Peter changed the word "afterward" to "in the last days," because he now realized the Messianic era, the last great moral epoch for the world, had begun, not by the Parousia, but by the outpouring of the Spirit.

And this outpouring of the Spirit had been given in order to prepare all mankind for the Parousia, the last coming of the Lord. Then "everyone shall be saved who calls upon the name of the Lord." Luke was the evangelist of the universality of salvation; so he has Peter say, that the Spirit was given to all mankind, and salvation to all who call on the name of the Lord, not just to the Jews.

Part 2 (2:22-36). Next, Peter proceeded to show that Jesus is truly risen from the dead. He used Scripture passages to do this. Then he concluded that because Jesus did rise from the dead, He is truly Lord and Messiah.

Boldly, completely indifferent about what others thought, Peter used the title "Jesus the Nazorean," a title scorned by the Jews.

This Jesus, the Nazorean, he told them, worked mighty deeds, wonders and signs, as foretold by Joel; but you killed Him, according to the plan and foreknowledge of God. Yet God raised him up from the throes of death, as David had prophesied long ago: "You will not abandon my soul to the nether world, nor will you suffer your holy one to see corruption." Peter pointed out that these words could not apply to David, for David's tomb in Jerusalem was a well-known landmark on Mt. Zion; whereas the tomb of Jesus was empty! And it was empty, because He is risen. Of this fact, we ourselves are witnesses.

Then Peter went on to state that this risen Jesus is divine, because David had written: "The Lord said to my Lord, sit at my right hand" (Ps. 109:1). Since, to sit at God's right hand means to share in what is a unique prerogative of God Himself, namely, universal Lordship of the universe, Peter had concluded that God had made Jesus both Lord and Messiah (Mt. 22:41-45). "Lord" was the word used for Yahweh when the Hebrew Scriptures was translated into Greek (the Septuagint). Messiah in Hebrew and *Christos* in Greek mean the Lord's anointed. Later, *Christos* became the surname of Jesus—Jesus Christ, the Lord's anointed.

David said all this, because Nathan had told him about a future Messiah (2 Sam 7:12-14). Peter proclaimed that that Messiah was Jesus.

Part 3 (2:37-41). Peter's discourse touched the people deeply. They cried out, "What are we to do?" Peter gave them three imperatives.

First, "Repent," he said; that is, change your minds about Jesus—He is God! Before ironing clothes, mother used to sprinkle them with water, so in ironing out our lives, the tears of repentance is the first step needed.

Secondly, Peter declared, "Be baptized in His name"; then you will receive the fire of the Holy Spirit who is offered to everyone, not just the Jews. Those who were baptized were about three thousand persons. (Note how faithful the apostles were to the last command of Christ, "Go, make disciples of all nations, baptizing them..." They did exactly that in Acts: first, they made disciples; then they baptized.)

Thirdly, he appealed, "Save yourselves from this corrupt generation." It is so easy "to go native." When white men went to the South Sea Islands, they were at first energetic and all get-up-and-go; but after some time, that energy died, that enthusiasm for work waned, and they began to become listless and easy-going. The natives then would say, "They have gone native"—have become just like the natives themselves. So with worldliness and the spirit of the world: at first we put up with it, then rationalize about it, then succumb to it, if we are not on the lookout. Alexander Pope put it this way:

> "Vice is a monster of such hideous mien,
> That to be hated, it needs but to be seen.
> Yet seen too oft, familiar with her face
> At first we *endure* , then *pity,* then *embrace.*"

Communal Life (2:42-47). The effect of Pentecost on the so-cial and liturgical life of the Church in Jerusalem was to create a community. The community had four elements.

First, it was very attentive to the teaching of the apostles (*didache*). This was not the same as the apostolic preaching (*kerygma*). Rather, it was the follow-up instructions given to the new converts after their conversion: make disciples (*kerygma*), baptize, teach (*didache*) (Mt. 28:19).

Secondly, the community practiced a sharing of their wealth together (*koinonia*). The Communist says, "All your property is mine." The Christian says, "All my property is yours."

Suppose a group of shipwrecked people were in a lifeboat. A steamer spots the lifeboat in the distance. However the steamer is carrying a precious cargo; time is of the essence. So the Captain feels he cannot stop, even for a lifeboat filled with people in des-perate need. Anyway, he reasons, it is not my business; moreover, I do not really know if they are need. So he keeps to his course. His neglect murdered those who died in the lifeboat. How much worse is it if souls are lost because of our neglect or unconcern for others!

Thirdly, this community sharing seemed to be tied in with the celebration of the Eucharist (the Breaking of the Bread). Love is the bond of unity; and the Eucharist is the source of love. Love gives. Love cares. Love shares. Then, too, the early Christians were well aware that it is in giving that we receive, that they could not hope for mercy unless they too showed mercy.

Fourthly, the community prayed, a very common practice in Judaism.

This primitive community disappears within a few years. In the famine of 48 A.D., the Jerusalem community was out of funds. So, appeals were made to the Gentile Church (1 Cor 8&9) to col-lect alms for the mother church in Jerusalem.

This sharing of earthly good was but a symbol of a deeper reality: their unity and their response to the commandment of Jesus to love one another as I have loved you.

Acts 3:1-26

3 Cure of a Crippled Beggar [1] Now Peter and John were going up to the temple area for the three o'clock hour of prayer. [2] And a man crippled from birth was carried and placed at the gate of the temple called "the Beautiful Gate" every day to beg for alms from the people who entered the temple. [3] When he saw Peter and John about to go into the temple he asked for alms. [4] But Peter looked intently at him, as did John, and said, "Look at us." [5] He paid attention to them, expecting to receive something from them. [6] Peter said, "I have neither silver nor gold, but what I do have I give you: in the name of Jesus Christ the Nazorean, [rise and] walk." [7] Then Peter took him by the right hand and raised him up, and immediately his feet and ankles grew strong. [8] He leaped up, stood, and walked around, and went into the temple with them, walking and jumping and praising God. [9] When all the people saw him walking and praising God, [10] they recognized him as the one who used to sit begging at the Beautiful Gate of the temple, and they were filled with amazement and astonishment at what had happened to him.

Peter's Speech [11] As he clung to Peter and John, all the people hurried in amazement toward them in the portico called "Solomon's Portico." [12] When Peter saw this, he addressed the people, "You Israelites, why are you amazed at this, and why do you look so intently at us as if we had made him walk by our own power or piety? [13] The God of Abraham, [the God] of Isaac, and [the God] of Jacob, the God of our ancestors, has glorified his servant Jesus whom *you handed over* and denied in Pilate's presence, when he had decided to release him. [14] *You denied* the Holy and Righteous One and asked that a murderer be released to you. [15] The author of life *you put to death,* but God raised him from the dead; of this we are witnesses. [16] And by faith in his name, this man, whom you see and know, his name has made strong, and the faith that comes through it has given him this perfect health, in the presence of all of you. [17] Now I know, brothers, that *you acted out of ignorance,* just as your leaders did; [18] but God has thus brought to fulfillment what he had announced *beforehand* through the mouth of all the prophets, that his *Messiah would suffer,* [19] Repent, therefore, and be converted, that your sins may be wiped away, [20] and that the Lord may grant you times of refreshment and send you the Messiah already appointed for you, Jesus, [21] whom heaven must receive until the times of universal restoration of which God spoke through the mouth of his holy prophets from of old. [22] For Moses said:

'A prophet like me will the Lord, your God,
      raise up for you
      from among your own kinsmen;
   to him you shall listen in all that he may say
      to you.
[23] Everyone who does not listen to that prophet
      will be cut off from the people.'

[24] Moreover, all the prophets who spoke, from Samuel and those afterwards, also announced these days. [25] You are the children of the prophets and of the covenant that God made with your ancestors when he said to Abraham, 'In your offspring all the families of the earth shall be blessed.' [26] *For you first,* God raised up his servant and sent him to bless you by turning each of you from your evil ways."

CHAPTER 3

Cure of a Crippled Beggar; Peter's Speech

In the next three chapters, Luke exemplifies "signs and wonders." In this chapter, the sign he uses is the cure of a man crippled since birth; the wonder he points out is that of a community of people who share.

Cure of a Crippled Beggar (3:1-10). The story of the cure of the crippled beggar was selected, not because it was one of Peter's more spectacular cures, but because it brought the apostles to the attention of the rulers and resulted in the first serious opposition to the church.

Peter and John are paired in this incident, and in the rest of Acts, even though John says and does nothing, because in Jewish law two witnesses were needed to testify to events, and because Jesus had instructed the apostles to travel in pairs (Lk. 10:1). Peter and John had been fishing partners; they had gone to the Baptist together; John got Peter into the high priest's house on the eve of Our Lord's passion; both went to the tomb on Easter; when Jesus told Peter of His destiny; Peter asked about John's (Jn. 21:21). Companions in the gospel; they remained companions in Acts.

Peter and John were going up to the temple to pray at three o'clock. How devout they were! The awesomeness of the coming of the Spirit did not cause them to relinquish their ordinary spiritual duties. Any vision that causes one to do that is suspect of not being from God.

The Jews prayed three times a day; very devout Jews would pray seven times a day (Ps. 119:164). The Jewish day began from 6:00 A.M. to 6:00 P.M. Hence the third, sixth and ninth hours were 9:00 A.M., noon, and 3:00 P.M. This Jewish practice shows how important it is that we have fixed times and places for prayers and devotions. The Church has based her Canonical Hours on the Jewish practice of praying seven times a day.

Well, every day at the hours of prayer, friends used to carry a man crippled from birth to the Gate called Beautiful, to beg for alms. Luke was a physician; he implied that the man's lameness was due to the weakness in and the malfunction of the ankle-bones. Therefore, crutches could not be used. He had to be carried.

The friends of the cripple used to carry him to the gate of the Temple, for they reasoned rightly that to worship God and be unconcerned about the plight of one's neighbor would be hypocrisy. Then, too, people went to the Temple to obtain God's blessings; they knew that only the merciful would obtain them—the hand open to give is in the best position to receive.

The beggar asked only for an alms; but he got far more than he had asked for. So often our prayers bring blessings far greater than those we had expected. "Silver and gold, I do not have," said Peter. "What I have I give you. In the name of Jesus Christ the Nazorean rise and walk."

Peter gave the cripple what no money could buy—his wholeness. Again the boldness of Peter, he used the despised title for Jesus, namely, "the Nazorean." And he dared to call Him the Christ, the anointed one, the Messiah, God! The man was instantly healed. Oh, the power of the name of Jesus! That same power is exercised daily in the sacraments, administered in the name of Jesus.

Look at a locomotive as it snorts, like a giant war-horse, in the station with a string of cars behind it. Now, no matter how powerful is that engine, it will not draw the cars behind itself unless the cars are coupled to it. Christ is the power, the locomotive, in the sacraments; our faith in them is the coupling link. Belief enabled the cripple to walk. Faith in the sacraments will enable us to walk to heaven.

Then, too, so many abuse the name of Christ in profanity—the name that made a cripple walk. How terribly tragic! At La Salette in 1846, Our Lady wept precisely because of profanity and the desecration of the Sunday. Such sins brought on the potato famine that took a million lives in Europe.

Such sins spawned the "Mad Year" of history—1848: the year that saw the birth of Karl Marx's creed "The Communist Manifesto"; the year in which De Rossi, the Secretary of State of Pope Pius IX, was stabbed to death and the Pope had to flee to Gaeta for his life; the year that Metternich rode out of Vienna to avoid being murdered; the year that Wellington was called out of retirement to quell the riots of London.

We can allegorize this miracle of the cure of the cripple. Let Peter and John, for instance, stand for the Church. The man lame from birth can symbolize all of us—born in sin. By her word and sacraments, the Church cures us of the ravages of sin. As the lame man stood by Peter and John when they were brought before the Sanhedrin, so we ought always be loyal to the Church which pours out upon us the blessings of her words and sacraments.

Peter's Speech (3:11-26). When Peter told the lame man to rise, he leaped up, stood for a moment to get the feel of standing on his own two legs, walked, then jumped and followed Peter and John into the Temple shouting and praising God.

The people were filled with amazement and astonishment. Their reaction was typical. They focused on the human healers rather than on God. Peter vehemently tried to correct this attitude. "Why do you look at us? We didn't do it! God did it to glorify His servant Jesus, whom you handed over and disowned in Pilate's presence."

Then he pointed out their sinfulness, not to condemn them, but to prick their consciences and to offer them grace, just as Jesus had always done. And so Peter did not spare them: "You handed Him over," he said; "you denied Him; you overrode Pilate's desire to set Him free; you preferred a murderer to Him; you killed Him!"

Then Peter made his pitch for their conversion. "But you acted out of ignorance. You didn't expect a suffering Messiah, even though the prophets had already foretold that (Ps. 21; Is. 53)." Then he went on, "Don't make the same mistake twice. Since Jesus has been raised from the dead, ignorance can no longer be an excuse. Repent, that is, change your minds; and be converted, that is, change your lifestyle." Repentance is negative: mourns for sins and repudiates them. Conversion is positive: turns to the Sinless One and accepts Him.

Brutus on the eve of the battle of Philippi argued for engaging in battle in these words:

> "There is a tide in the affairs of men,
> Which taken at the flood, leads on to fortune.
> Omitted, all the voyage of their life is bound
> in shallows and in miseries."

Brutus was telling Cassius that it's now or never. If a ship is beached on the seashore, it must take the tide when it comes in or else remain stranded. Peter was telling his listeners the same thing: "Repent and be converted"—now! Now is the acceptable time!

Peter appealed for repentance and conversion for two reasons. First, regarding the past, "That your sins may be wiped away." The words "wiped away" are vivid. The ancients wrote on papyrus and the ink they used had no acid in it. Therefore it didn't bite into the papyrus as modern ink does. It simply lays on top of it. Hence to erase a writing, all a person had to do was to take a wet sponge and simply wipe it away. As easily, sin is wiped away when one repents.

Secondly, Peter appealed for repentance, regarding the future, "that the Lord may grant you times of refreshment." Conversion brings love, peace, joy into one's life.

Repentance and conversion prepare for the coming of the Lord. Christianity is linear: it is going somewhere. Paganism is cyclic: it goes around in circles, goes nowhere. Hence Christianity is a romance, for it has purpose. Paganism is boredom, for it has no purpose. If you drive your car and have someplace to go, you do not mind the drive. But if you are made to drive your car in circles around a lot for no reason whatsoever, it will drive you mad.

Finally, Peter made it crystal clear that Christianity is not a rejection of Judaism, but its fulfillment. Those people who reject Christ cut themselves off from God's people. Those Jews who rejected Christ were the first Protestants.

"God raised up his Servant (Is 53)," Peter informed them, in order "to bless you by turning each of you from your evil ways." You would think that God after the Jews had crucified His Son would have nothing more to do with His people. Or if he raised up His Son, it would have been only to send Him to take revenge. Yet He did none of these things. Instead, He raised up His Son to bless them; and the greatest blessing is to turn one away from sin.

Christ alone meets man's greatest need, which is deliverance from sin. You might just as well try to put out Vesuvius with a teaspoonful of cold water or try to catch a whale with a fishhook or a crocodile with a silken thread, as to try to cure the sickness of humanity without grappling with sin. Christ did just that. He killed the power of sin by dying on the cross. *Per crucem ad lucem*—Through the cross to the light. (Cp., Browning's "Apparent Failure")

Without sin, life would be joyous. Oscar Wilde called sin "sweet sin." Sweet only for the moment, but followed by terrible remorse. The greatest blessing God can give us is to turn us from our evil ways.

Acts 4:1-37

4 [1] While they were still speaking to the people, the priests, the captain of the temple guard, and the Sadducees confronted them [2] disturbed that they were teaching the people and proclaiming in Jesus the resurrection of the dead. [3] They laid hands on them and put them in custody until the next day, since it was already evening. [4] But many of those who heard the word came to believe and [the] number of men grew to [about] five thousand.

Before the Sanhedrin [5] On the next day, their leaders, elders, and scribes, were assembled in Jerusalem, [6] with Annas the high priest, Caiaphas, John, Alexander, and all who were of the *high priestly class.* [7] They brought them into their presence and questioned them, "By what power or by what name have you done this?" [8] Then Peter, filled with the Holy Spirit, answered them, "Leaders of the people and elders. [9] If we are being examined today about a good deed done to a cripple, namely, by what means he was saved, [10] then all of you and all the people of Israel should know that it was in the name of Jesus Christ the Nazorean whom you crucified, whom God raised from the dead; in his name this man stands before you healed. [11] He is 'the stone rejected by you, the builders, which has become the cornerstone.' [12] There is no salvation through anyone else, nor is there any other name under heaven given to the human race by which we are to be saved."

[13] Observing the boldness of Peter and John and perceiving them to be uneducated, ordinary men, they were amazed, and they recognized them as the companions of Jesus. [14] Then when they saw the man who had been cured standing there with them, they could say nothing in reply. [15] So they ordered them to leave the Sanhedrin, and conferred with one another, saying, [16] "What are we to do with these men? Everyone living in Jerusalem knows that a remarkable sign was done through them, and we cannot deny it. [17] But so that it may not be spread any further among the

people, let us give them a stern warning never again to speak to anyone in this name."

¹⁸ So they called them back and ordered them not to speak or teach at all in the name of Jesus. ¹⁹ Peter and John, however, said to them in reply, "Whether it is right in the *sight of God for us to obey you rather than God,* you be the judges. ²⁰ It is impossible for us not to speak about what we have seen and heard." ²¹ After threatening them further, they released them, finding no way to punish them, on account of the people who were all praising God for what had happened. ²² For the man on whom this sign of healing had been done *was over forty years old.*

Prayer of the Community ²³ After their release they went back to their own people and reported what the chief priests and elders had told them. ²⁴ And when they heard it, they raised their voices to God with one accord and said, "Sovereign Lord maker of heaven and earth and the sea and all that is in them, ²⁵ you said by the Holy Spirit through the mouth of our father David, your servant:

'Why did the Gentiles rage
  and the peoples entertain folly?
²⁶ The Kings of the earth took their stand
  and the princes gathered together
    against the Lord and against his anointed.'

²⁷ Indeed they gathered in this city against your holy servant Jesus whom you anointed, Herod and Pontius Pilate, together with the Gentiles and the peoples of Israel, ²⁸ to do what your hand and [your] will had long ago planned to take place. ²⁹ And now, Lord, take not of their threats, and enable your servants to speak your word with all boldness, ³⁰ as you stretch forth [your] hand to heal, and signs and wonders are done through the name of your holy servant Jesus." ³¹ As they prayed, the place where they were gathered shook, and *they were filled with the Holy Spirit,* and continued to speak the word of God with *boldness.*

Life in the Christian Community [32] The community of believers was of one heart and mind, and no one claimed that any of his possessions was his own, but they had everything in common. [33] With great power the apostles bore witness to the resurrection of the Lord Jesus, and great favor was accorded them all. [34] There was no needy person among them, for those who owned property or houses would sell them, bring the proceeds of the sale, [35] and put them at the feet of the apostles, and they were distributed to each according to need. [36] Thus Joseph, also named by the apostles Barnabas (which is translated "son of encouragement"), a Levite, a *Cypriot by birth,* [37] sold a piece of property that he owned, then brought the money and put it at the feet of the apostles.

CHAPTER 4

Break with Judaism Begins

This chapter focuses on the conflict between the Sanhedrin, the old leaders of the Jewish people, and the apostles, the new leaders; and it shows a shift in leadership from the old (the Sanhedrin) to the new (the Apostles).

The cure of the lame man took place around 3:00 P.M. After the miracle, Peter and John preached for about three hours, for "it was already evening" when the temple guard and the Sadducees confronted them.

As with Jesus, the reaction of religious officialdom was unfavorable—not to the cure, but to Peter's preaching about the resurrection of Jesus. The Sadducees in particular were hostile, because they did not believe in the resurrection (Mt. 22:23, 33; Acts 23:8). Their hostility was to escalate until it led to the martyrdom of Stephen.

The reaction of the people, on the contrary, was more positive. Many were converted — "the number of men grew to about five thousand."

Simple folk, you see, are more susceptible to the supernatural than the learned. For learning puffs up, causes pride and prejudice. But simple folk just look to the facts. They reason: these men did good works; therefore their words must also be good. Jesus once praised His Father because He hid things from the wise and learned, but "revealed them to the childlike" (Matt. 11:25).

Because the Sanhedrin did not meet at night, Peter and John were arrested and put in jail until the next day.

The reason for their arrest was their teaching. Christianity is a teaching religion. It rests on facts, not opinion; on historical events, not on the thoughts of some philosopher.

The priests persecuted them, because they felt the apostles were usurping their teaching prerogative; the temple guard persecuted them, because the guards were sycophants, who went along with the upper crust just to hold on to their jobs; and the Sadduccees persecuted them, because their denial of the resurrection was being challenged.

Before the Sanhedrin (4:5-22). The tribunal of the Sanhedrin was formidable: Annas, Caiaphas, John, Alexander, and others. The opposition was centered in one family. How important is the family for good or for evil!

When persons of humble station are faced by such an august body, usually they either cringe in cowardice or display brazen insolence. But not Peter and John; they acted with courtesy, with dignity, and fearlessly. For Jesus had forewarned them, "When they hand you over, do not worry about how you are to speak or what you are to say. You will be given at that moment what you are to say. For it will not be you who speak but the Spirit..." (Mt. 10:19-20).

The Sanhedrin opened their case against Peter and John by asking, "By what power or name have you done this?"

Peter answered that it was "in the name of Jesus Christ the Nazorean whom you crucified, whom God raised from the dead..." Then Peter, under the Holy Spirit, stated that Christianity is not just one among other religions; rather, "There is no salvation through anyone else, nor is there any other name under heaven given to the human race by which we are to be saved."

The Sanhedrin were confounded by the boldness and learning of the apostles. Then the cured cripple was also there: against a fact no argument is valid. Incidentally, how brave and grateful the cripple was to come before such a formidable body to back up his benefactors! The Sanhedrin were perplexed, so they ordered the accused out of court while they got their heads together. "What are we to do?" they said to each other. How sad! Instead of facing the evidence and accepting it, they blinded themselves. They called the apostles back and told them not to teach at all in the name of Jesus.

Again, Peter responded boldly, "It is not right to obey you and disobey God. It is impossible for us not to speak about what we have seen and heard."

Luke shows here that the old religious leaders have forfeited their claims as the religious leaders of the nation, by their rejecting the Messiah sent by God. Since these leaders were disobeying God, the apostles, and the peoples, no longer owed them obedience. For to obey them would mean to disobey God.

The apostles replaced them as the new leaders of God's people. Jesus, the Jewish Messiah, had appointed them. The Church was taking shape.

To see a child in danger in the road and do nothing is wrong. To see a house on fire and say nothing is wrong. Truth cannot be kept to oneself without sin. One must speak out. For evil to succeed, it is enough for good men to do nothing. The apostles refused to be silent.

They were dismissed, but with further warning. On this occasion, nothing worse happened to them, because the Sanhedrin feared the people and feared what the crippled man might say, for he was more than 40 years old and so could talk for himself.

The impotence of the enemies of Christ. You may shake your fist at the sun in order to darken the world; stamp you foot on the seashore to repel the tide; tell the wind not to blow. But to no avail. In the play, *My Fair Lady,* Eliza Doolittle sings about the conceited Mr. Higgins: "England will still be England without you; the world will still spin without you." So hell's gates will never prevail against God's Church. With or without the Sanhedrin, the Church will prosper. Man proposes; but God disposes.

Prayer of the Community (4:23-31). After their trouble, Peter and John went back to the Church: to their support community. God's people did two things. They sought comfort in Scripture; and they prayed, not for deliverance, but for the power to speak the word with boldness and with signs and wonders. In answer to their prayers, the Holy Spirit came once again upon them (a 2nd Pentecost). Then the earth shook to symbolize that their teachings would shake and shape the world.

Life in the Christian Community (4:32-37). As always, the effect of the coming of the Spirit is unity; "the community of believers was of one heart and mind." This unity extended itself even to the common sharing of goods — "they had everything in common." This detachment from material goods gave great credibility to their preaching of the resurrection.

However, this common sharing of goods was purely local, voluntary and temporary. Some Christians gave all they had to the community chest; others sold possessions from time to time as special needs for relief arose; still others kept their property in social trust—that is, when needs arose, they were quite willing to sell some of their property and lay the money at the feet of the apostles.

As usual, Luke gives two illustrations of this charity. First, there was a certain Levite from the island of Cyprus, named Joseph. He was honest and liberal. He sold a farm he owned and gave the proceeds to the apostles. They changed his name to Barnabas. Then there was Ananias and Sapphira. They were dishonest and greedy. Luke tells their story in the next chapter.

Acts 5:1-42

5 Ananias and Sapphira [1] A man named Ananias, however, with his wife Sapphira, sold a piece of property. [2] He retained for himself, with his wife's knowledge, some of the purchase price, took the remainder, and put it at the feet of the apostles. [3] But Peter said, "Ananias, why has Satan filled your heart so that you lied to the Holy Spirit and retained part of the price of the land? [4] While it remained unsold, did it not remain yours? And when it was sold, was it not still under your control? Why did you contrive this deed? You have lied not to human beings, but to God." [5] When Ananias heard these words, he fell down and breathed his last, and great fear came upon all who heard of it. [6] The young men came and wrapped him up, then carried him out and buried him.

[7] After an interval of about three hours, his wife came in, unaware of what had happened. [8] Peter said to her, "Tell me, did you sell the land for this amount?" She answered, "Yes, for that amount." [9] Then Peter said to her, "Why did you agree to test the Spirit of the Lord? Listen, the footsteps of those who have buried your husband are at the door, and they will carry you out." [10] At once, she fell down at his feet and breathed her last. When the young men entered they found her dead, so they carried her out and buried her beside her husband. [11] And great fear came upon the whole church and upon all who heard of these things.

Signs and Wonders of the Apostles [12] Many signs and wonders were done among the people at the hands of the apostles. They were all together in Solomon's portico. [13] None of the others dared to join them, but the people esteemed them. [14] Yet more than ever, believers in the Lord, great numbers of men and woman, were added to them. [15] Thus they even carried the sick out into the streets and laid them on cots and mats so that when Peter came by, at least his shadow might fall on one or another of them. [16] A large number of people from the towns in the vicinity of Jerusalem also gathered, bringing the sick and those disturbed by unclean spirits, and they were all cured.

Trial before the Sanhedrin. [17] Then the high priest rose up and all his companions, that is, the party of the Sadducees, and filled with jealousy, [18] laid hands upon the apostles and put them in the public jail. [19] But during the night, the angel of the Lord opened the doors of the prison, led them out, and said, [20] "Go and take your place in the temple area, and tell the people everything about this life." [21] When they heard this, they went to the temple early in the morning and taught. When the high priest and his companions arrived, they convened the Sanhedrin, the full senate of the Israelites and sent to the jail to have them brought in. [22] But the court officers who went did not find them in the prison, so they came back and reported. [23] "We found the jail securely locked and the guards stationed outside the doors, but when we opened them, we found no one inside." [24] When they heard this report, the captain of the temple guard and the chief priests were at a loss about them, as to what this would come to. [25] Then someone came in and reported to them, "The men whom you put in prison are in the temple area and are teaching the people." [26] Then the captain and the court officers went and brought them in, but without force, because they were afraid of being stoned by the people.

[27] When they had brought them in and made them stand before the Sanhedrin, the high priest questioned them, [28] "We gave you strict orders [did we not?] to stop teaching in *that name.* Yet you have filled Jerusalem with your teaching and want to bring *this man's* blood upon us." [29] But Peter and the apostles said in reply, *"We must obey God rather than men.* [30] The God of our ancestors raised Jesus, *though you had him killed by hanging him on a tree.*

[31] God exalted him at his right hand as leader and savior to grant Israel repentance and forgiveness of sins. [32] We are witnesses of these things, as is the Holy Spirit that God has given to those who obey him."

[33] When they heard this, they became infuriated and wanted to put them to death. [34] But a Pharisee in the Sanhedrin named Gamaliel, a teacher of the law, respected by all the people, stood up, ordered the men to be put out-

side for a short time, [35] and said to them, "Fellow Israelites, be careful what you are about to do to these men. [36] Some time ago, Theudas appeared, claiming to be someone important, and about four hundred men joined him, but he was killed, and all those who were loyal to him were disbanded and came to nothing. [37] After him came Judas the Galilean at the time of the census. He also drew people after him, but he too perished and all who were loyal to him were scattered. [38] So now I tell you, have nothing to do with these men, and let them go. For if this endeavor or this activity is of human origin, it will destroy itself. [39] But if it comes from God, you will not be able to destroy them; you may even find yourselves fighting against God." They were persuaded by him. [40] After recalling the apostles, they had them flogged, ordered them to stop speaking in the name of Jesus, and dismissed them. [41] So they left the presence of the Sanhedrin, rejoicing that they had been found worthy to suffer dishonor for the sake of the name. [42] And all day long, both at the temple and in their homes, they did not stop teaching and proclaiming the Messiah, Jesus.

CHAPTER 5

Unity of Community Threatened

Ananias and Sapphira (5:1-11). Since persecution from without had only strengthened the Christian community, Satan began to work from within the community. All he ever needs to hurt the Church is one or two "pious" church members. Ananias means "grace of God"; and Sapphira signifies sapphire, a brilliant jewel.

Satan filled their hearts. The devil goes away from a closed door; but he enters open doors, that is, empty hearts.

Ananias and Sapphira had opened the doors of their hearts to Satan by being deceitful and greedy. Their evil was not in holding back money; for no one was compelled to give—giving was voluntary. Their evil consisted in their deceit and their greed. They both actually lied; and they both pretended to give all they had to the Church, so that they would be able to draw continually on the poor fund.

But worst of all, they wanted to test the Spirit, to see if the Spirit was with the apostles. Thus Peter asked Sapphira, "Why did you agree to test the Spirit of the Lord?" They actually had their doubts about the apostles.

Because of the great danger this presented to the community, The Holy Spirit acted dramatically and caused them both to die on the spot. A wholesome fear, as a result, came upon all.

Still, this deception had a very bad effect on the community. Before Ananias and Sapphira had sinned, there was a beautiful sharing of goods in the community. "There was no needy person among them" (4:24). But after their sin, this never happens again.

Instead, the poor have to rely on charity— "their widows were being neglected" (6:1). Ananias and Sapphira weakened trust and confidence in the charitable works of the early Church. Hence the seriousness of their sin.

Christianity never advocated that everybody toss everything into a common pool and live on it. The right of private property is a basic natural right, stemming from the right to life. Because I have a right to life, I have a right to those things necessary for life, like food, clothing and shelter. But in using these things, I destroy them. Therefore I have a right to things with the power to destroy them, which is what is meant by private property. Atheistic Communism denies this right. The Church defends this right. Her Religious Orders are no denial of this right, for religious common life is only for the few who consecrate their lives to God by the vows of poverty, obedience and chastity.

Signs and Wonders of the Apostles (5:12-16). From the particular Ananias incident, Luke goes to the general. Many other signs and wonders were done among the people at the hands of the apostles. To eliminate any idea of magic, these miracles were worked in Solomon's portico, where the cripple man had been cured in the name of Jesus, and so not by magic. These cures were so prolific that people came from the towns in the vicinity of Jerusalem. Even Peter's shadow healed. Some feared to join them because of the Sanhedrin; but great numbers believed and were added to the Church. All esteemed them.

When Peter came by, people put their sick in the streets so that his shadow might fall on them. So too our lives cast shadows. Everyone of use exerts an influence on all upon whom our "shadow" falls: a quiet influence, but real; perhaps unconscious but factual. Every act, word, look, attitude of ours is a force on those with whom we rub elbows that either builds up or tears down.

Our shadow tags behind us. So the evil or good we do lives after us. This is true of great lives and of humble lives. The roar of Niagara can be heard farther away, but it is not sweeter than the ripple of the brook. The Alps is a sign of God's power, but the violet is a sign of His goodness. The eagle may soar higher, but the canary has a sweeter song. The penny of the widow was greater than the gold of the rich.

In a word, every life is important. Life invests us with great responsibility. Strive to exert a beneficent influence. "You are the light of the world." We are our brother's keeper. The influence of the good in the past has helped us: we worship in churches that others built, go to schools others constructed, enjoy a freedom others fought for, we owe it to them to pass on our Christian heritage to our children.

Then, too, we might learn from the simplicity of the people: what faith they had to think a shadow could cure. And it did. We go to Mass: but there, there is more than a shadow—there is the risen Lord Himself. Perhaps we are not helped so much by the Mass, because we do not have the simple faith of those who believed the shadow of an apostle could heal the ills of body and soul. Cats on hot days seek the shade; so in the heat of life, we ought to seek the shade of the divine presence at Mass—the shadow of His wings.

Trial before the Sanhedrin(5:17-42). The conflict between the old and the new leaders of the Jewish people came to a head when the high priest, with the party of the Sadducees, arrested the apostles out of envy. They envied their popularity and their unlimited healing powers. Luke shows that God is on the side of the apostles, because at night the angel of the Lord (the Sadducees denied the existence of angels) freed them from prison saying, "Go into the temple area and tell the people everything about this life."

The gospel is called "life." It gives the Holy Spirit who creates new life in being and in becoming. This new life causes sinful habits to drop off the soul, just as in springtime the rising life within the tree causes the withered leaves to drop to the earth; the tender shoots put forth dislodge the dead leaves which all winter may have defied the strongest winds that had tried to tear them from the boughs.

When the Sanhedrin convened in the morning, the apostles were in the temple preaching. How obedient they are! How fearless! The people were in the temple for the morning sacrifice, but not the Sanhedrin. They did not practice their faith. The apostles were preaching in public; the Sanhedrin were plotting in private.

When the Sanhedrin had convened, they sent for the apostles who had been sent to jail. They were perplexed at not finding them there. When someone informed them that the apostles were in the temple area, guards were sent to bring them to trial.

The twelve were accused of contempt of court. They had been told not to teach in that name— "you ...want to bring *this man's* blood upon us." Note how the enemies of Jesus avoided mentioning His name. They feared its power. Hence hell prompts people to abuse that name in profanity.

Again Peter spoke up for all. What a defense he made! In a nutshell, he told them, "We must obey God rather than men. This God raised the Jesus you killed from the dead. This Jesus is at the right hand of God to save all by forgiving the sins of all who repent. We are witnesses of this, as is the Holy Spirit who is given to all who obey him."

Instead of repenting, the Sanhedrin became infuriated. They wanted to put them to death. But Gamaliel, a teacher of the law, respected by all people, ordered the apostles to be put outside for a short time.

Among the Jews there were two schools of thought: the conservative school of Shammai and the liberal one of Hillel. Gamaleil was the grandson of Hillel and a liberal. He permitted his students to study Greek literature; taught that those engaged in works of mercy should be exempt from strict Sabbath laws; bade his disciples to greet pagans on feast days with "Peace be to you." Therefore, the people loved and respected him. Gamaliel was one of the seven Jewish doctors honored with the title "Rabban." He was the teacher of St. Paul. He died in 60 A.D.

Well, this Gamaliel got up and came to the defense of the apostles. He reflected on how in the past religious leaders had come and had died, and their religions had died with them.Then he made this marvelous statement: "If this endeavor...is of human origin, it will destroy itself. But if it comes from God, you will not be able to destroy them; you may even find yourselves fighting against God."

So Gamaliel advocated moderation, a wait-and-see policy, when all the while the Sanhedrin should have been weighing the evidence to get at the truth.

What about other religions that have lasted? Is mere age decisive? The religion of Egypt lasted 3000 years—but it is dead now. Brahmanism and Buddhism are old, but are they not dead—they do not grow? Mohammedanism did spread for a while—but by the sword.

Christianity has had no such history. Christ preached the cross. He sent his disciples as sheep among wolves. In the Garden, He told Peter to put up his sword.

Christ was a Jew; He embraced a divine religion, Judaism. And from Judaism came Christianity—came as the apple comes out of the bud and the blossom. Yet Jews crucified Christ—these were the first "protestants." But a remnant, at least ten or 12 thousand of them, entered the Church; among these the great rabbi Saul, Paul.

When I talk to Jews, I tell them jokingly that they are in the wrong church. I tell them that we have the temple, the sacrifice, the priesthood. All you have, I remind them, is your synagogue— a school of learning.

This Christianity, the offspring of Judaism, was preached to the four corners of the earth and took root in a Greco-Roman civilization. The tiny seed grew into a tree, sheltering two to three million Christians. St. Justin Martyr wrote in her defense. Lucan and Celsus wrote against her.

Then terrible persecutions assailed her. Nero and Domitian attacked her in the first century for personal reasons. In the second and third centuries, some Roman Emperors began to believe that the old Roman religion was necessary for the welfare of the State. So men, like Marcus Aurelius, Decius, Diocletian, persecuted the Church. But in the end the Church won. "Thou has conquered, O pale Galilaen," cried the dying Julian the Apostate (+363).

Then in the fifth century, came the Teutonic Barbarian in the German forest. Their first evangelists were Christian captives. Missionaries followed, like Patrick to Ireland, Austin to England, Boniface to Germany, Remigius to the Franks, Ansgar to Norway, Cyril and Methodius to the Slavs. Within a few centuries, the Dark Ages gave way to the Christian civilization of Europe (over 80 million).

Still it marches on. The Renaissance and Reformation came, she weathered these. Today the clash is with Secular Humanism. So she convoked Vatican II to renew herself and to bring hearts, homes, parishes, nations, back to God. As Gamaliel had foretold, "If this be the work of man, it would have been dead and buried centuries ago." His inference has to be right: it must be of God.

The Sanhedrin took only half of Gamaliel's advice. They flogged the apostles, ordered them to stop speaking in the name of

Jesus, and dismissed them. The apostles left the Sanhedrin rejoicing that they had been found worthy to suffer for the sake of the name. And all day long, both in the temple and in their homes, they did not stop teaching and proclaiming that Jesus is the Messiah.

This section of Acts, chapters 1 to 5, ends with the helplessness of the old leaders of God's people, the Sanhedrin, and the unstoppable preaching of the new, the apostles. The Church is born!

Acts 6:1-8:3

6 The Need for Assistants [1] At that time, as the number of disciples continued to grow, the Hellenists complained against the Hebrews because their widows were being neglected in the daily distribution. [2] So the Twelve called together the community of the disciples and said, "It is not right for us to neglect the word of God to serve at table. [3] Brothers, select from among you seven reputable men, filled with the Spirit and wisdom, whom we shall appoint to this task, [4] whereas we shall devote ourselves in prayer and to the ministry of the word." [5] The proposal was acceptable to the whole community, so they chose Stephen, a man filled with faith and the Holy Spirit, also Philip, Prochorus, Nicanor, Timon, Parmenas, and Nicholas of Antioch, a convert to Judaism. [6] They presented these men to the apostles who prayed and laid hands on them. [7] The word of God continued to spread, and the number of the disciples in Jerusalem increased greatly; even a large group of priests were becoming obedient to the faith.

Accusation against Stephen [8] Now Stephen, filled with grace and power, was working great wonders and signs among the people. [9] Certain members of the so-called Synagogue of Freedmen, Cyrenians, and Alexandrians, and people from Cilicia and Asia came forward and debated with Stephen, [10] but they could not withstand the wisdom and the spirit with which he spoke. [11] Then they instigated some men to say, "We have heard him speaking blasphemous words against Moses and God." [12] They stirred up the people, the elders, and the scribes, accosted him, seized him, and brought him before the Sanhedrin. [13] They presented false witnesses who testified, "This man never stops saying things against [this] holy place and the law. [14] For we have heard him claim that this Jesus the Nazorean, will destroy this place and change the customs that Moses handed down to us." [15] All those who sat in the Sanhedrin looked intently at him and saw that his face was like the face of an angel.

7 Stephen's Discourses. [1] Then the high priest asked, "Is this so?" [2] And he replied, "My brothers and fathers, listen, The God of glory appeared to our father Abraham while he was in Mesopotamia, before he had settled in Haran, [3] and said to him '*Go forth from your land and [from] your kinsfolk to the land that I will show you.*' [4] So he went forth from the land of the Chaldeans and settled in Haran. And from there, after his father died, he made him migrate to this land where you now dwell. [5] Yet he gave him no inheritance in it, not even a foot's length, but he did promise to give it to him and his descendants as a possession, even though he was childless. [6] And God spoke thus, 'His descendants shall be aliens in a land not their own, where they shall be enslaved, and oppressed for four hundred years; [7] but I will bring judgment on the nation they serve,' God said, ' and after that they will come out and worship me in this place.' [8] Then he gave him the covenant of circumcision, and so he became the father of Isaac, and circumcised him on the eighth day, and Isaac did Jacob, and Jacob the twelve patriarchs.

[9] "And the patriarchs, jealous of Joseph, sold him into slavery in Egypt, but God was with him, [10] and rescued him from all his afflictions. He granted him favor and wisdom before Pharaoh, the king of Egypt, who put him in charge of Egypt and [of] his entire household. [11] Then a famine and great affliction struck all Egypt and Canaan, and our ancestors could find no food; [12] but when Jacob heard that there was grain in Egypt, he sent our ancestors there a first time. [13] The second time, Joseph made himself known to his brothers, and Joseph's family became known to Pharaoh. [14] Then Joseph sent for his father Jacob, inviting him and his whole clan, seventy-five persons, [15] and Jacob went down to Egypt. And he and our ancestors died [16] and were brought back to Shechem and placed in the tomb that Abraham had purchased for a sum of money from the sons of Hamor at Shechem.

[17] "When the time drew near for the fulfillment of the promise that God pledged to Abraham, the people had increased and become very numerous in Egypt, [18] until an-

other king who knew nothing of Joseph came to power [in Egypt]. [19] He dealt shrewdly with our people and oppressed [our] ancestors by forcing them to expose their infants, that they might not survive. [20] At this time Moses was born, and he was extremely beautiful. For three months he was nursed in his father's house, [21] but when he was exposed, Pharaoh's daughter adopted him and brought him up as her own son. [22] Moses was educated with all the wisdom of the Egyptians and was powerful in his words and deeds.

[23] "When he was forty years old, he decided to visit his kinsfolk, the Israelites. [24] When he saw one of them treated unjustly, he defended and avenged the oppressed man by striking down the Egyptian. [25] He assumed [his] kinsfolk would understand that God was offering them deliverance through him, but they did not understand. [26] The next day he appeared to them as they were fighting and tried to reconcile them peacefully, saying, 'Men you are brothers. Why are you harming one another?' [27] Then the one who was harming his neighbor pushed him aside, saying, 'Who appointed you ruler and judge over us? [28] Are you thinking of killing me as you killed the Egyptian yesterday?' [29] Moses fled when he heard this and settled as an alien in the land of Midian, where he became the father of two sons.

[30] "Forty years later, an angel appeared to him in the desert near Mount Sinai in the flame of a burning bush. [31] When Moses saw it he was amazed at the sight, and as he drew near to look at it, the voice of the Lord came. [32] 'I am the God of your fathers, the God of Abraham, of Isaac, and of Jacob.' Then Moses, trembling, did not dare to look at it. [33] But the Lord said to him, 'Remove the sandals from your feet, for the place where you stand is holy ground. [34] I have witnessed the affliction of my people in Egypt and have heard their groaning, and I have come down to rescue them. Come now, I will send you to Egypt.' [35] This Moses, whom they had rejected with the words, 'Who appointed you ruler and judge?' God sent as [both] ruler and deliverer, through the angel who appeared to him in the bush. [36] This man led them out, performing wonders and signs in the land of Egypt,

at the Red Sea, and in the desert for forty years. [37] It was this Moses who said to the Israelites, 'God will raise up for you, from among your own kinsfolk, a prophet like me.' [38] It was he who, in the assembly in the desert, was with the angel who spoke to him on Mount Sinai and with our ancestors, and he received living utterances to hand on to us.

[39] "Our ancestors were unwilling to obey him; instead, they pushed him aside and in their hearts turned back to Egypt, [40] saying to Aaron, 'Make us gods who will be our leaders. As for that Moses who led us out of the land of Egypt, we do not know what has happened to him.'

[41] So they made a calf in those days, offered sacrifice to the idol, and reveled in the works of their hands. [42] Then God turned and handed them over to worship the host of heaven, as it is written in the book of prophets:

> "Did you bring be sacrifices and offerings
> > for forty years in the desert, O house of
> > > Israel?
> [43] No, you took up the tent of Moloch
> and the star of [your] god Rephan,
> > the images that you made to worship.
> So I shall take you into exile beyond
> > Babylon.'

[44] "Our ancestors had the tent of testimony in the desert just as the One who spoke to Moses directed him to make it according to the pattern he had seen. [45] Our ancestors who inherited it brought it with Joshua when they dispossessed the nations that God drove out from before our ancestors, up to the time of David, [46] who found favor in the sight of God and asked that he might find a dwelling place for the house of Jacob. [47] But Solomon built a house for him. [48] Yet the Most High does not dwell in houses made by human hands. As the prophet says:

> [49] 'The heavens are my throne,
> > the earth is my footstool.

> What kind of house can you build for me?
> says the Lord,
> Of what is to be my resting place?
> [50] Did not my hand make all these things?'

Conclusion [51] "You stiff-necked people, uncircumcised in heart and ears, you always oppose the Holy Spirit; you are just like your ancestors. [52] Which of the prophets did your ancestors not persecute? They put to death those who foretold the coming of the righteous one, whose betrayers and murderers you have now become. [53] You received the law as transmitted by angels, but you did not observe it."

Stephen's Martyrdom [54] When they heard this, they were infuriated, and they ground their teeth at him. [55] But he, filled with the Holy Spirit, looked up intently to heaven and saw the glory of God and Jesus standing at the right hand of God, [56] and he said, "Behold, I see the heavens opened and the Son of Man standing at the right hand of God." [57] But they cried out in a loud voice, covered their ears, and rushed upon him together. [58] They threw him out of the city , and began to stone him. The witnesses laid down their cloaks at the feet of a young man named Saul. [59] As they were stoning Stephen, he called out, "Lord Jesus. receive my spirit." [60] Then he fell to his knees and cried out in a loud voice, "Lord, do not hold this sin against them"; and when he said this he fell asleep.

8 [1] Now Saul was consenting to his execution.

Persecution of the Church. On that day, there broke out a severe persecution of the church in Jerusalem, and all were scattered throughout the countryside of Judea and Samaria, except the apostles. [2] Devout men buried Stephen and made a loud lament over him. [3] Saul, meanwhile, was trying to destroy the church; entering house after house and dragging out men and women, he handed them over for imprisonment.

CHAPTER 6

Persecution in Jerusalem Spreads the Church

In the new Church there were two kinds of Jews. There were the Palestinian or Hebrew Jews and the Foreign or Hellenistic Jews. The distinction came about as a result of the Jewish Captivities. Before the Assyrian (721 B.C.) and Babylonian (606 B.C.) Captivities the Jews were alone; after these Captivities, they were scattered all over the then-known world, from India to the Aegean.

The number that returned from Babylon under Zorababel and Ezra were far less than those who stayed behind. These Jews who had returned home, because of the Captivity experience, recoiled from contact with pagans. They grew narrower in their outlook, more exclusive and proud.

The Jews who did not return but remained among the pagans, from their prolonged contact with them, were naturally affected: they greatly modified their customs and modes of thought. This was especially true after the wars of Alexander the Great (333 B.C.). He imposed the Grecian culture; and as a result, a spirit of secularism entered into their lives and broke down their apartness—the hallmark of Judaism. A new spirit of commercial enterprise awoke within them and they began to become the bankers of the world. Cut off from the Temple and its sacrifice, the dispersed Jews had recourse to the Bible and the synagogue and developed a religion in spirit and in truth.

When Christianity arose and began to spread among the nations, it used the synagogues of the Hellenistic Jews as its first base of operations. It was from these Hellenized Jews that the Church got some of her best missionaries, like Stephen, Philip, and Nicholas. And thanks to them too, she was able to break out of the danger of Judaic exclusivism to become the religion of all mankind.

The Palestinian or Hebrew Jews took pride in their orthodoxy and tended to look down on their countrymen who had become Hellenized. They felt that they had become contaminated by Grecian culture. The Hellenistic Jews, on the contrary, tended to view their stay-at-home, old-fashioned brothers as ignorant, intolerant and bigoted.

The antagonism between the two groups showed itself in the doling out of alms to the needy. The Hellenistic Jews felt that their widows were being discriminated against by the Hebrew or Palestinian Jews. They murmured.

The Need for Assistant (6:1-7). The Twelve evidenced their leadership in the community be addressing this problem themselves. This resulted in the creation of the office of deacons. By meeting each need and solving each problem as it arose, the early Church grew hierarchically. It was a grassroots growth. Such growing is far better than superimposing an already elaborated structure from without. When the growth is from within, to meet a present need, then it will be organic and tightly knit. It was in this way that the early church grew.

The people named seven men "to serve at table." They were called "deacons," for "deacon" means "a servant." These men were appointed to take care of the temporalities of the church. From their names, it is obvious that they were all Hellenistic Jews. So the murmuring (an evil) brought great good. It brought into the hierarchy of the Church its most free, spiritual, un-Hebrew and catholic elements. One man especially was destined to infuriate the narrow, ultra-national party of the Pharisees; his death occasioned the scattering of the Church from Jerusalem. That man was Stephen. He was the first to see that Christianity was more encompassing than Judaism and was meant for all the world. His death led to the conversion of the Apostle of the Gentiles—Saul!

In administrating temporalities, men should be "filled with the Spirit and wisdom"—for relief should be personal and sympathetic, not institutional nor mechanical. It requires discrimination and care, lest the truly needy be neglected and the undeserving be helped. Relief, too, is not the sum and substance of Christian charity. Two of the seven selected were men of the Spirit—Stephen and Philip. They bore testimony to Christ by their lives and preaching.

The upshot of all this was that the faith increased. This was due partly to the seven, partly because the apostles had more time to preach and pray, and partly because the dissension in the Christian community had been removed. "The word of God continued to spread and the number of disciples in Jerusalem increased greatly."

Accusation Against Stephen (6:8-15). Stephen filled with grace and power worked signs and wonders among the people. Stephen had a vision of a world for Christ. He saw that the Temple must pass away and that the Law was but a step to the gospel. He said so—even in the synagogue of the Hellenists.

Such assertions started a veritable donnybrook. Stephen was challenged. Some of his opponents were from Cilicia. Tarsus is the capital of Cilicia and was the home of Saul. So, very likely, Saul was in on the debate. But the Hellenists were no match for Stephen. He outargued them. His face shone like the face of an angel. As a light in a vase makes it translucent, so the Spirit in Stephen transformed him, emitting an ethereal glow.

Saul was deeply impressed. In fact, he was so touched that at the stoning of Stephen, he refrained from joining them. Instead, he simply looked on, watching over the cloaks laid at his feet by those stoning Stephen. Grace was beginning to work in him.

Stephen's Discourse (7:1-53). Stephen's defense is an intercalation, an insertion. Before, only the Sadducees opposed the Church; now all did: the Pharisees out of jealousy, the people out of a misguided zeal.

In his defense, Stephen gave a rapid survey of the history of Israel from Abraham to the death of Jesus. The world thinks kings and statesmen make history: Stephen and men of faith believe God does. The value of history is not so much what it tells of the past, as what it tells of God: His character, His ethics, His relationship to man!

Salvation History is linear, not cyclic, as for the pagan. It is going somewhere, pointing to Christ. But most of the Jews refused to go.

In Stephen's speech, there are many inaccuracies. But that is understandable, for Stephen was talking off the cuff in very trying circumstances. Moreover, Stephen was interested in the broad sweep of things, just as an artist sacrifices many details for the over-all impression.

In his defense, Stephen showed that the great men of Israel were men of faith. They had heard God's command and were not afraid to obey it even though it meant change—even though it meant becoming displaced persons.

So it was with Abraham. "Go forth from your land and from your kinsfolk," God said. And Abraham went forth, not knowing where he was going (Heb. 11:8).

So it was with Joseph. When his brothers feared that after the death of their father, Jacob, Joseph might revenge himself on them, Joseph reminded them that he saw things as God saw them. "Even though you meant harm for me, God meant it for good..."(Gn. 50:20).

Finally, there was Moses. He gave up being Pharaoh of Egypt just to do what God wanted him to do, namely, to lead His people. The actions of the Sanhedrin, Stephen implied, were in sharp contrast to those of their ancestors. "You," Stephen concluded, "have but one desire: to keep things as they were and to regard Jesus and His followers as dangerous innovators."

Secondly, Stephen pointed out that men worshipped God long before there was a holy land or Temple; for instance, in the 40-year desert experience. Therefore, the holy land and the Temple are relative.

Then Stephen concluded in anger, crying out: "You stiff-necked people...you always oppose the Holy Spirit. When you crucified Jesus, you were simply acting out your national heritage: your ancestors did not obey Moses; and they turned to false gods—a calf, Moloch, and star gods. And you are no better!"

In philosophy we say, "Against a fact no argument is valid." Stephen had stated the facts. There could be only one response: Stephen's death. As St. Augustine said on the feast of John the

Baptist: *"Veritas parit odium."* "Truth begets hate." Hatred begot death for both John and Stephen.

Stephen died about 36 A.D. Pilate had been summoned to Rome about that time, so that the supreme power over life and death was in the hands of the Sanhedrin.

Stephen saw Jesus standing at the right hand of God, not sitting, for the Church was in great need so Jesus stood, ready to help.

Truth *forever* on the scaffold, Wrong forever on the throne—
Yet that scaffold sways the future, and, behind the dim unknown,
Standeth God within the shadow, keeping watch above his own.

Persecution of the Church (8:2-3). Stephen was the proto-martyr, the first martyr in the Church. Luke parallels his death with the death of Christ. Both prayed for their persecutors; both commended themselves to God; both died outside the walls of Jerusalem. St. Augustine said that the prayer of Stephen changed Saul to Paul. "Had Stephen not prayed; Paul had not preached." How irresistible is the power of prayer and example!

Stephen's death signaled a fierce persecution of the Church in Jerusalem. This served only to scatter the sparks of truth and enkindle the fires of the gospel elsewhere—in the countryside of Jerusalem and Samaria. The blood of martyrs is a seed.[1]

---

[1]   Pontius Pilate, on one of his characteristic fits of exasperation, ordered the massacre of a group of harmless Samaritan pilgrims at the foot of their holy mountain, Gerizim. Vitellius, legate of Syria, deposed Pilate December 36 A.D. and sent him to Rome to answer to the Emperor for his injustice.

When he reached Rome, Tiberius had died on March 16, 37 A.D., and Caligula was the new emperor. Because of the sea travel, there was a lapse in appointing a successor to Pilate. During this brief interim, the Sanhedrin resumed their power to execute without the approval of Rome.

They promptly tried Stephen and stoned him to death in May 37 A.D. Then they sent Saul in late summer to Damascus to hunt down Christians.

Facts on Acts

Acts 3:4-40

III. The Mission in Judea and Samaria

Ch.8

Philip in Samaria [4] Now those who had been scattered went about preaching the word. [5] Thus Philip went down to [the] city of Samaria and proclaimed the Messiah to them. [6] With one accord, the crowds paid attention to what was said by Philip when they heard it and saw the signs he was doing. [7] For unclean spirits, crying out in a loud voice, came out of many possessed people, and many paralyzed and crippled people were cured. [8] There was great joy in that city.

Simon the Magician [9] A man named Simon used to practice magic in the city and astounded the people of Samaria, claiming to be someone great. [10] All of them, from the least to the greatest, paid attention to him saying, "This man is the 'Power of God' that is called 'Great.'" [11] They paid attention to him because he had astounded them by his magic for a long time, [12] but once they began to believe Philip as he preached the good news about the kingdom of God and the name of Jesus Christ, men and women alike were baptized. [13] Even Simon himself believed and, after being baptized, became devoted to Philip; and when he saw the signs and mighty deed that were occurring, he was astounded.

[14] Now when the apostles in Jerusalem heard that Samaria had accepted the word of God, they sent them Peter and John, [15] who went down and prayed for them, that they might received the Holy Spirit, [16] for it had not yet fallen upon any of them; they had only been baptized in the name of the Lord Jesus. [17] Then they laid hands on them and they received the Holy Spirit.

[18] When Simon saw that the Spirit was conferred by the laying on of the apostles' hands, he offered them money [19] and said, "Give me this power too, so that anyone upon whom I lay my hands may receive the Holy Spirit." [20] But Peter said to him, "May your money perish with you, be-

cause you thought that you could buy the gift of God with money. [21] You have no share or lot in this matter, for your heart is not upright before God. [22] Repent of this wickedness of yours and pray to the Lord that, if possible, your intention may be forgiven. [23] For I see that you are filled with bitter gall and are in the bonds of iniquity." [24] Simon said in reply, "Pray for me to the Lord, that nothing of what you have said may come upon me." [25] So when they had testified and proclaimed the words of the Lord, they returned to Jerusalem and preached the good news to many Samaritan villages.

Philip and the Ethiopian [26] Then the angel of the Lord spoke to Philip, "Get up and head south on the road that goes down from Jerusalem to Gaza, the desert route." [27] So he got up and set out. Now there was an Ethiopian eunuch, a court official of the Candace, that is, the queen of the Ethiopians, in charge of her entire treasury, who had come to Jerusalem to worship, [28] and was returning home. Seated in his chariot, he was reading the prophet Isaiah. [29] The Spirit said to Philip, "Go and join up with that chariot" [30] Philip ran up and heard him reading Isaiah the prophet and said, "Do you understand what you are reading?" [31] He replied, "How can I, unless someone instructs me?" So he invited Philip to get in and sit with him. [32] This was the scripture passage he was reading:

> "Like a sheep he was led to the slaughter
>> and as a lamb before its shearer is silent,
>>> so he opened not his mouth.
> [33] In [his] humiliation justice was denied him.
>> Who will tell of his posterity?
>> For his life is taken from the earth"

[34] Then the eunuch said to Philip in reply, "I beg you, about whom is the prophet saying this? About himself, or about someone else?" [35] Then Philip opened his mouth and, beginning with this scripture passage, he proclaimed Jesus to

him. [36] As they traveled along the road they came to some water, and the eunuch said, "Look there is water. What is to prevent my being baptized?" [37] [38] Then he ordered the chariot to stop, and Philip and the eunuch both went down into the water, and he baptized him. [39] When they came out of the water, the Spirit of the Lord snatched Philip away, and the eunuch saw him no more, but continued on his way rejoicing. [40] Philip came to Azotus, and went about proclaiming the good news to all the towns until he reached Caesarea.

Facts on Acts

CHAPTER 7

The Broadening of the Church

The first seven chapters of Acts show how the Church was shaping up. It was growing, but it was still centered in Jerusalem and was Jewish-centered. The next five chapters (8-12) describe a period of transition: the gospel is carried out of Jerusalem and Judea and the foundations are laid for carrying it to the ends of the earth. The great names in these chapters are Philip, Saul, Cornelius and Peter.

The persecution following upon St. Stephen's martyrdom drove Christians out of Jerusalem. It takes a storm to scatter the winged seeds hither and thither where they will germinate and bear fruit far from the parent tree. "All were scattered throughout the countryside of Judea and Samaria, except the apostles."

The apostles did not leave Jerusalem after the martyrdom of St. Stephen. Generals often have to stand still in the center of the battle to direct their forces; or when a ship is sinking, officers and crew remain with it to the last. So the apostles stayed in Jerusalem. Perhaps, too, the persecution was limited to the Hellenistic Christians and did not affect the Hebrew Christians, whose attitude toward the law and the temple was more in line with Judaism.

Philip in Samaria (8:4-8). Stephen is dead; Philip takes his place. That is the military rule. As it was Stephen who articulated that the Church was to be missionary, open to all; so it was Philip who became the first missionary, so much so, that he was nicknamed "the Evangelist" (Acts 21:8). Philip went to the city of Samaria and proclaimed the gospel to the Samaritans.

The Samaritans were Judaised Gentiles, just as the Hellenists were Gentilised Jews. So they were the natural bridge between Jew and Gentile.

In the eighth century B.C., Assyria conquered the Northern Kingdom of Israel of which Samaria was the capital. Its inhabitants were transported to Assyria and colonists from the East were sent in to occupy the deserted land. Intermarriage resulted with those left behind in Palestine. This mixed race was called the Samaritans. Racial purity was lost—an unforgivable crime for Jews.

Moreover, wild animals began to terrorize the land. The strangers attributed this to the anger of the local deity, of whose worship they were ignorant. So the king of Assyria sent Jewish priests to instruct them in religious rites. Since the Bible had not yet been assembled, the Samaritans accepted only the five books of Moses from the Scriptures. Thus the Samaritans became a hybrid race with a hybrid religion (2 Kings 17:24-41).

In the sixth century, the Babylonians conquered the Southern Kingdom whose capital was Jerusalem. As was the custom in those days, the people were transported to Babylon. But they stubbornly refused to lose their identity and remained Jews. When they came back to Jerusalem in the fifth century, the Samaritans offered to help them rebuild their city and temple. The help was contemptuously refused, because they were not pure Jews. The Samaritans reacted by erecting a temple of their own on Mt. Gerizim around 420 B.C. (Ezra 4). Later, John Hyrcanus (134-104 B.C.) destroyed this temple on Mt. Gerizim.

This bitter history bred a deep enmity between the two nations, so much so that the name Samaritan became a byword of reproach among the Jews. You can well imagine, then, how miraculous it was to have a Jew preaching to the Samaritans and the Samaritans listening to a Jew.

In Our Lord's time the Samaritans retained their worship on Gerizim, though the temple was in ruins. As the Samaritan woman disclosed to Jesus, they had some vague expectations of a Messiah.

Simon the Magician (8:9-25). From the incident of Our Lord with the Samaritan woman, it seems the Samaritans were a simple people with a childlike taste for the marvelous, and an equally childlike credulity (John 4). Such a simple, childlike people were wide open to magic. When Philip came to them, they were under the spell of a certain magician, Simon Magus. He had bewitched them. But when Philip came working wonders, Simon was himself bewitched. Simon regarded Philip only as a magician like himself, but greater; and his baptism as a magical rite. Simon's wonders produced only fear; but Philip's healed and helped. Simon sought his own glory; Philip sought Christ's glory. Simon spoke to their eyes; Philip appealed to their hearts. Philip worked great signs; driving out demons, curing the paralyzed and crippled. So, "there was great joy in that city."

The joy reached fever pitch not only because of the many cures at no cost, but because they saw God's hand there and began to realize what God really is—One who cared even for the despised Samaritans. They therefore had grounds for future hope.

True religion benefits not only man's soul, but also his body. True religion heightens everything it touches. Lord Bacon wrote: "There never was found in any age of the world either philosophy or sect or law or discipline which could so rightly exalt the public good as the Christian faith."

Philip was so successful that the apostles in Jerusalem sent Peter and John to Samaria (38 A.D.). Here we have the classic text for the sacrament of confirmation (Acts 8:14-17). The Samaritans had been baptized in the name of the Lord Jesus. Philip was only a deacon. So two bishops were sent, Peter and John. And they prayed that the Samaritans might receive the Holy Spirit. After praying, they laid hands on them, and they received the Holy Spirit. John, the son of thunder, who once had asked Jesus to send down fire upon Samaria, now invokes another flame that enkindles, but does not consume.

This Samaritan incident showed that in the early church there was a hierarchy (apostles who could lay on hands and deacons who could preach, but not lay on hands) and a rite supplementary to baptism, conferred by one with special authority, through prayer and the laying on of hands, to effect a fuller communication of the Holy Spirit. Furthermore, this giving of the Holy Spirit showed that God confirmed Philip's preaching of the gospel to non-Jews, the Samaritans! This was a great advance in the spreading of the gospel.

Philip was so successful in Samaria, because Christ had prepared the way years before with the Samaritan woman and because the Samaritans had received Jesus: one grace accepted brings others upon its heel.

"When Simon saw that the Spirit was conferred by the laying on of the apostles' hands, he offered them money." Some people think money can buy anything. This sign appeared at a kennel: "Puppy love—the only love money can buy." Later on, the attempt to buy spiritual offices or powers was called "Simony" after Simon Magus.

Peter reacted decisively to Simon's offer of money. He had already seen in Judas and in Ananias and Sapphira what a love of money can do. So he cursed Simon and warned him of destruction if he did not repent and pray. Simon did not pray. Instead, he asked Peter to pray for him; and what he asked for was not a change of heart, but a warding off of the evil consequences that might stem from his actions.

Fish sometimes leap out of the water with great energy, but it would be foolish to conclude that they are leaving the water for good. In a moment they are back in the water as though they had never left it. What tempted the fish to leap out of the water was but a fly—the water is still its home. So Simon leaped into the Church, had been baptized by Philip, but only for monetary gain; not obtaining it, he fell back into his old ways. Simon became one of the founders of the weird far-flung heresy which became known in the next century as Gnosticism.

Philip and the Ethiopian (8:26-40). Perhaps Philip was a bit downcast by the relapse of Simon Magus. He had received him into the Church and Peter had uncovered his evilness. Lest Philip become discouraged, an angel of the Lord came to him and told him to "head south on the road that goes down from Jerusalem to Gaza, the desert route." Obediently, Philip got up, left busy Samaria where he had been a great success, and set out for a desert road, 60 miles long, ending in the haughty, wicked city of Gaza.

On this road there was an Ethiopian eunuch, a court official, the treasurer of the Candace, Amintare, the famed queen of Ethiopia (now Sudan) Ethiopians—and so a man of great influence. He had come to Jerusalem to worship and was returning home.

As we had mentioned earlier, at this time the world was full of people weary of the many gods and the loose morals of the nations. In this fullness of time, many of them turned to Judaism with its one God and austere moral standards that gave life meaning. They attended the synagogues and read the Scriptures, but did not consider themselves bound by other regulations, such as circumcision and the observance of dietary laws. They were God-fearers. Jews of the Dispersion had no doubt brought their faith to this far-off land. The eunuch was perhaps one of their converts, for he had come a long way to Jerusalem to worship in the Court of the Gentiles. He was a student of the Scriptures. Seated in his chariot, he was reading the prophet Isaiah, who had made mention of his country and had prophesied that one day its people would worship the true God.

The Spirit said to Philip, "Go join up with that chariot." Philip ran and heard the eunuch reading aloud the prophet Isaiah. Philip asked him, "Do you understand what you are reading?" How humble was the eunuch and how eager to learn. "How can I," he answered, "unless someone instructs me." And he invited Philip into his chariot. Scripture needs an interpreter.

Speaking before King William of Orange, a preacher chose this text and said it had four subjects of astonishment: first, a courtier was reading Scripture; secondly, a courtier admitted ignorance; thirdly, a courtier asked an inferior to instruct him; and lastly, the courtier was converted.

The eunuch was pondering the meaning of Isaiah 53:7-8, a passage that Christianity from its earliest origins, has applied to Jesus. This Chapter 53 on the Suffering Servant of God was one of the most often quoted Old Testament passages by Christians to prove Jesus had to suffer.

When the eunuch became a believer, he was baptized. As early as this, baptism was seen as the first step in admitting Gentiles to Christianity.

Tradition has it that this eunuch went home and became the apostle of Ethiopia. From the viewpoint of salvation, all souls are equal. But from the viewpoint of missionary strategy, all men are not equal. It is more important to win a man of great influence and power, who can afterwards win thousands to the faith, than the rank-and-file who may become very fine Christians, but who have little influence and cannot change the state of things.

Norway was won for Christ by winning King Olaf. Hungary was won by the conversion of St. Stephen. The Franks by the baptism of Clovis. So, the Spirit led Philip to the eunuch, a man of great influence, in order to lead Ethiopia to the Lord.

Likewise, today, we must win rulers, and political, economic, scientific, artistic personalities. They are the engineers of souls. They lead and influence. Win them and you win the people.

This fascinating narrative is freighted with other practical lessons for evangelization.

First of all, opportunities are found in the most unexpected places. Whoever would have thought that the apostle of Africa would have been found on a deserted road to Gaza. But for those who follow divine guidance, who are open to the Spirit, unexpected surprises are in store.

Philip was a man of the Spirit. The Spirit speaks, Philip runs. Opportunities are fleeting. Tide and time wait for no man, neither does the Spirit. God demands instant obedience. Joseph gave it when he was told to "take the child and his mother and flee into Egypt." The rich young man did not; and as far as we know Jesus never gave him another chance.

Again, God always works at both ends of the line. The Spirit inspires Philip to go to the chariot of the eunuch. He moves the eunuch to read the 53rd chapter of the Prophet Isaiah. He always prepares the way for His evangelizers.

This incident manifests the principle of supernaturality. It is not enough to be religious. The Ethiopian was a religious man, so were Saul and Cornelius. Yet God intervened in their lives to give them the fullness of truth. To those who live according to the light they have, more light will be given. God wills all men to come to the fullness of truth.

After the baptism of the eunuch, the Spirit of the Lord snatched Philip away. He went from town to town till he came to Caesarea, probably his own hometown. Twenty-four years later, when St. Paul comes to Caesarea (Acts 21:8-9), he stayed at Philip's home. By this time Philip was known only as the evangelist. With him his four daughters lived—all virgins who had the gift of prophecy. St.

Luke probably knew Philip personally. A Greek tradition says that Philip later left Caesarea and became bishop of Tralles in Lydia. We have no date concerning this great man's death. He was in on the beginnings of the deaconate, of confirmation, and was the first to receive half-Jews, the Samaritans, and a Gentile, the Ethiopian eunuch, into the Church. His feast is celebrated June 6.

Facts on Acts

Acts 9:1-43

9 Saul's Conversion [1] Now Saul, still breathing murderous threats against the disciples of the Lord, went to the high priest [2] and asked him for letters to the synagogues in Damascus, that, if he should find any men or women who belonged to the Way he might bring them back to Jerusalem in chains. [3] On his journey, as he was nearing Damascus, a light from the sky suddenly flashed around him. [4] He fell to the ground and heard a voice saying to him. *"Saul, Saul, why are you persecuting me?"* [5] He said, *"Who are you, sir?"* The reply came, *"I am Jesus, whom you are persecuting.* [6] Now get up and go into the city and you will be told what you must do."* [7] The men who were traveling with him stood speechless, for they heard the voice but could see no one. [8] Saul got up from the ground, but when he opened his eyes he could see nothing: so they led him by the hand and brought him to Damascus. [9] For three days he was unable to see, and he neither ate nor drank.

Saul's Baptism [10] There was a disciple in Damascas named Ananias, and the Lord said to him in a vision, "Ananias." He answered, "Here I am Lord." [11] The Lord said to him, "Get up and go to the street called Straight and ask at the house of Judas for a man from Tarsus named Saul. He is there praying, [12] and [in a vision] he has seen a man named Ananias come in and lay [his] hands on him, that he may regain his sight." [13] But Ananias replied, "Lord, I have heard from many sources about this man, what evil things he has done to your holy ones in Jerusalem. [14] And here he has authority from the chief priests to imprison all who call upon your name." [15] But the Lord said to him, "Go, for this man is *a chosen instrument of mine to carry my name before Gentiles, kings, and Israelites,* [16] and I will show him what he *will have to suffer for my name."* [17] So Ananias went and entered the house, laying his hands on him, he said, "Saul, my brother, the Lord has sent me, Jesus who appeared to you on the way by which you came, that you may regain your sight and be filled with the Holy Spirit."

[18] Immediately things like scales fell from his eyes and he regained his sight. He got up and was baptized, [19] and when he had eaten he recovered his strength.

Saul Preaches in Damascus *He stayed some days with the disciples in Damascus,* [20] and he began at once to proclaim Jesus in the synagogues, that he is the Son of God. [21] All who heard him were astounded and said, "Is not this the man who in Jerusalem ravaged those who call upon this name, and came here expressly to take them back in chains to the chief priests?" [22] But Saul grew all the stronger and confounded [the] Jews who lived in Damascus, proving that this is the Messiah.

Saul Visits Jerusalem [23] *After a long time had passed,* the Jews conspired to kill him, [24] but their plot became known to Saul. Now they were keeping watch on the gates day and night so as to kill him, [25] but his disciples took him one night and let him down through an opening in the wall, lowering him in a basket.

[26] When he arrived in Jerusalem he tried to join the disciples, but they were all afraid of him, not believing that he was a disciple. [27] Then Barnabas took charge of him and brought him to the apostles, and he reported to them how on the way he had seen the Lord and that he had spoken to him, and how in Damascus he had spoken out boldly in the name of Jesus. [28] He moved about freely with them in Jerusalem, and spoke out boldly in the name of the Lord. [29] He also spoke and debated with the Hellenists, but they tried to kill him. [30] And when the brothers learned of this, they took him down to Caesarea and sent him on his way to Tarsus.

The Church at Peace [31] The church throughout all Judea, Galilee and Samaria was at peace. It was being built up and walked in the fear of the Lord, and with the consolation of the Holy Spirit it grew in numbers.

Peter Heals Aeneas at Lydda [32] As Peter was passing though every region, he went down to the holy ones living in Lydda. [33] There he found a man named Aeneas, who had been confined to bed for eight years, for he was paralyzed. [34] Peter said to him, "Aeneas, Jesus Christ heals you. Get up and make your bed." He got up at once. [35] And all the inhabitants of Lydda and Sharon saw him, and they turned to the Lord.

Peter Restores Tabitha to Life. [36] Now in Joppa there was a disciple named Tabitha (which translated means Dorcas). She was completely occupied with good deeds and almsgiving. [37] Now during those days she fell sick and died, so after washing her, they laid [her] out in a room upstairs. [38] Since Lydda was near Joppa, the disciples, hearing that Peter was there, sent two men to him with the request, "Please come to us without delay." [39] So Peter got up and went with them. When he arrived, they took him to the room upstairs where all the widows came to him weeping and showing him the tunics and cloaks that Dorcas had made while she was with them. [40] Peter sent them all out and knelt down and prayed. Then he turned to her body and said, "Tabitha, rise up." She opened her eyes, saw Peter, and sat up. [41] He gave her his hand and raised her up, and when he had called the holy ones and the widows, he presented her alive. [42] This became known all over Joppa, and many came to believe in the Lord. [43] And he stayed a long time in Joppa with Simon, a tanner.

IV The Inauguration of The Gentile Mission

10 The Vision of Cornelius [1] Now in Caesarea there was a man named Cornelius, a centurion of the Cohort called the Italica, [2] devout and God-fearing along with his whole house-hold, who used to give alms generously to the Jewish people and pray to God constantly. [3] One afternoon about three o'clock, he saw plainly in a vision and angel of God come in to him and say to him, "Cornelius." [4] He looked intently at him, and seized with fear, said, "What is it, sir?" He said to him, "Your prayers and almsgiving had ascended as a memorial offering before God. [5] Now send some men to Joppa and summon one Simon who is called Peter. [6] He is staying with another Simon, a tanner, who has a house by the sea." [7] When the angel who spoke to him had left, he called two of his servants and a devout soldier from his staff, [8] explained everything to them, and sent them to Joppa.

The Vision of Peter [9] The next day, while they were on their way and nearing the city, Peter went up to the roof terrace to pray at about noontime. [10] He was hungry and wished to eat, and while they were making preparations he fell into a trance. [11] He saw heaven opened and something resembling a large sheet coming down, lowered to the ground by its four corners. [12] In it were all the earth's four-legged animals and reptiles and the birds of the sky. [13] A voice said to him, "Get up, Peter. Slaughter and eat." [14] But Peter said, "Certainly not, sir. For never have I eaten anything profane and unclean." [15] The voice spoke to him again, a second time, "What God has made clean, you are not to call profane." [16] This happened three times, and then the object was taken up into the sky.

[17] While Peter was in doubt about the meaning of the vision he had seen, the men sent by Cornelius asked for Simon's house and arrived at the entrance. [18] They called out inquiring whether Simon, who is called Peter, was staying there. [19] As Peter was pondering the vision, the Spirit said [to him], "There are three men here looking for you. [20] So get up, go downstairs, and accompany them without hesitation, because I have sent them." [21] Then Peter went down to the men and said, "I am the one you are looking for. What is the reason for your being here?" [22] They answered, "Cornelius, a centurion, an upright and God-fearing man, respected by the whole Jewish nation, was directed by a holy angel to summon you to his house and to hear what you have to say." [23] So he invited them in and showed them hospitality.

The next day he got up and went with them, and some of the brothers from Joppa went with him. [24] On the following day he entered Caesarea. Cornelius was expecting them and had called together his relatives and close friends. [25] When Peter entered, Cornelius met him and, falling at his feet, paid him homage. [26] Peter, however, raised him up, saying, "Get up. I myself am also a human being." [27] While he conversed with him, he went in and found many people gathered together [28] and said to them, "You know that it is unlawful for a Jewish man to associate with, or visit, a Gentile, but God has shown me that I should not call any person profane or unclean [29] And that is why I came without objection when sent for. May I ask, then, why you summoned me?"

[30] Cornelius replied, "Four days ago at this hour, three o'clock in the afternoon, I was at prayer in my house when suddenly a man in dazzling robes stood before me and said, [31] 'Cornelius, your prayer has been heard and your almsgiving remembered before God. [32] Send therefore to Joppa and summon Simon, who is called Peter. He is a guest in the house of Simon, a tanner, by the sea.' [33] So I sent for you immediately, and you were kind enough to come. Now therefore we are all here in the presence of God to listen to all that you have been commanded by the Lord."

Peter's Speech [34] Then Peter proceeded to speak and said, "In truth, I see that God shows no partiality. [35] Rather, in every nation whoever fears him and acts uprightly is acceptable to him. [36] You know the word [that] he sent to the Israelites as he proclaimed peace through Jesus Christ, who is Lord of all, [37] what has happened all over Judea, beginning in Galilee after the baptism that John preached, [38] how *God anointed Jesus of Nazareth with the Holy Spirit and power.* He went about doing good and healing all those oppressed by the devil, for God was with him. [39] *We are* witnesses of all that he did both in the country of the Jews and [in] Jerusalem. They put him to death by hanging him on a tree. [40] This man God raised [on] the third day and granted that he be visible, [41] not to all the people, but to us, the witnesses chosen by God in advance, who ate and drank with him after he rose from the dead. [42] He commissioned us to preach to the people and testify that he is the one appointed by God as judge of the living and the dead. [43] To him all the prophets bear witness, that everyone who believes in him will receive forgiveness of sins through his name."

11 The Baptism of the Gentiles Explained [1] Now the apostles and the brothers who were in Judea heard that the

Gentiles too had accepted the word of God. [2] So when Peter went up to Jerusalem the circumcised believers confronted him, [3] saying, "You entered the house of the uncircumcised people and ate with them." [4] Peter began and explained it to them step by step, saying, [5] "I was at prayer in the city of Joppa when in a trance I had a vision, something resembling a large sheet coming down, lowered from the sky by its four corners, and it came to me. [6] Looking intently into it, I observed and saw the four-legged animals of the earth, the wild beasts, the reptiles, and the birds of the sky. [7] I also heard a voice say to me, 'Get up, Peter. Slaughter and eat.' [8] But I said, 'Certainly not, sir, because nothing profane or unclean has ever entered my mouth.' [9] But a second time a voice from heaven answered, 'What God has made clean, you are not to call profane.' [10] This happened three times, and then everything was drawn up again into the sky. [11] Just then three men appeared at the house where we were, who had been sent to me from Caesarea. [12] The Spirit told me to accompany them without discriminating. These six brothers also went with men, and we entered the man's house. [13] He related to us how he had seen [the] angel standing in his house, saying, 'Send someone to Joppa and summon Simon, who is called Peter, [14] who will speak words to you by which you and all your household will be saved.' [15] As I began to speak, the Holy Spirit fell upon them as it had upon us at the beginning, [16] and I remembered the Word of the Lord, how he had said, ' John baptized with water but you will be baptized with the Holy Spirit.' [17] If then God gave them the same gift he gave to us when we came to believe in the Lord Jesus Christ, who was I to be able to hinder God?" [18] When they heard this, they stopped objecting and glorified God, saying, "God has then granted life-giving repentance to the Gentiles too."

CHAPTER 8

Readying the Church for the Gentiles

Preparing an apostle for the Gentiles. In the vacuum of authority left by the death of Tiberius (March 16, 37 A.D.), and the coming of Caligula, the Sanhedrin exerted its power even outside of Judea. They sent the avid persecutor, Saul, in the summer of 37, to the Syrian city of Damascus to hunt down Christians. On the road, Saul was converted.

His conversion, so dramatically narrated in Acts 9:1-9, is repeated two times more in Acts 22:3-16 and 26:12-18. That Luke should narrate this conversion three times is testimony to the importance he attached to it.

All three accounts differ in details with the exception of the dialogue between Christ and Paul. Here there is full verbal agreement in all three accounts.

"Saul, Saul, why are you persecuting me?"

"Who are you, sir?"

"I am Jesus whom you are persecuting."

Why this word-for-word repetition? Because these words exerted a profound and lasting influence on the thought of Paul. In his conversion experience, he discovered that the Church he was persecuting was identified with Christ as body to head. In persecuting the Church, he was stepping on her toe, and lo and behold, who complains but Christ. You step on one's toe and the head cries

"Ouch!" Thus Paul came to liken the Church to the body of Christ, the mystical body of Christ, and Christ as her Head (1Corinthians 12:27).

Another reason for Luke giving three accounts of Saul's conversion was to silence those Jews and Judaizers who challenged Paul's right to evangelize the Gentiles. Again and again, he was attacked as having no right to preach the word of God, since he was not one of the Twelve (Galatians 1:11-23; 2 Corinthians 3). To defend Paul's mission to the Gentiles, Luke had to prove beyond the shadow of a doubt that Paul was every bit an apostle, well qualified for the mission, and hand-picked by Jesus just as the other Twelve were.

Therefore, in the first account of Saul's conversion, in Greek, Luke shows that Paul really saw Christ. In the second account, in Aramaic, Luke shows that Paul alone of all the apostles had seen the glorified Christ. In the third account, in Greek, Luke shows Paul as prophet and servant of Yahweh.

Saul's Conversion (9:1-9). One of the greatest arguments for the truth of the Christian faith is the conversion of Saul. How explain Paul, unless he were converted? And how explain his conversion unless Christ had truly risen from the dead and proven Himself divine?

The conversion of Saul was one of the sequels to Stephen's martyrdom. Ever since Saul saw the face of Stephen glow like the face of an angel, he could hardly live with himself. Apparently an inner conflict had been going on within him for a long time, as the remark "it is hard for you to kick against the goad" (Acts 26:14) implied.

Saul tried to kick against the goad by feverish activity against the Church. His guilt expressed itself in his hostility against the disciples of the Lord. Later on, his cruelty in persecuting the Church haunted him. "I persecuted the church of God beyond measure and tried to destroy it." (Galatians 1:13).

Saul's fervent persecution of the Church in Jerusalem had forced her underground; but refugees were reported to have reached Damascus, spreading "the Way" there. The fact that Saul received letters from the high priest "to the synagogues in Damascus" showed that Jewish leaders still considered Christians as a Jewish sect, and so under their jurisdiction. Apparently, too, Christians in Damascus were still going to the synagogues, as those in Jerusalem still went to the Temple. The fact that Ananias is able to go to the house of Judas, a highly respected Jew, to whom Saul was brought, shows that outside of Jerusalem Jews and Christians got along pretty well.

Damascus is 140 miles northeast of Jerusalem. The journey from Jerusalem takes several days. Saul, as a result, had much time to think; and his thoughts disturbed him greatly. When he neared the city, he was inwardly in terrible turmoil.

Saul was one of those rare men—sincere and honest. He hunted down the Christians because he honestly believed they were God's enemies. He sought no personal glory, no reward. He was dedicated to God, and so God gave him a tremendous grace; on the road, "a light from the sky suddenly flashed around him." He fell to the ground. Then a voice, clear as a bell, said to him, "Saul, Saul, why are you persecuting me?" His traveling companions also heard the thunderous voice, but they could see no one—a proof Saul wasn't dreaming or hearing things. Yet not one of them was affected as was Saul.

God strikes one down only to lift up. So to Saul, the voice said, "Get up and go into the city." When he arose from the ground and opened his eyes, he could see nothing. He was blind—blinded by the light of glory shining on the face of Christ.

Though blinded by the light of glory, yet Saul had received the light of faith (an inner grace). He had heard the voice of God and it told him, "Go into the city and it will be told you what to do." Docile and believing Saul had his companions lead him by hand into the city. Later on, Paul could write to the Romans that "faith comes from what is heard" (Romans 10:17).

He was so shaken by the experience, that he could eat nothing for three days.

Saul's Baptism (9:10-19a). God, as we have seen in the case of Philip and the eunuch, always prepares people for the gospel by working at both ends. He had spoken to Saul; now He would speak to Ananias. He told Ananias to go to Straight Street to the house of Judas and lay hands on Saul of Tarsus, for "he is there praying." Prayer is the mark of genuine conversion. You can always trust a praying man. Yet Ananias remonstrated because Saul's reputation had gone on before him. The Lord insisted, "Go, for I have chosen him to carry my name before the Gentiles and to suffer for my name." We serve God not only by what we do but also by what we suffer. Life is action and passion. When Paul reflects on his life, it is always his sufferings he lists (2 Corinthians 11:16-29).

Ananias yielded, went, laid hands on Saul, called him "brother," restored his sight and filled him with the Holy Spirit.

Saul got up and was baptized July or August 37 A.D.

Saul preaches in Damascus (9:19b-22). For a few weeks, Paul preached Christ in the synagogues of Damascus, astounding Jews and Christians alike. The Jews plotted to kill him, so he fled for a time into Arabia (Gal. 1:17). He probably stayed there less than a year; then he returned to Damascus for almost two years (38-40 A.D.).

Saul visits Jerusalem (9:23-30). "After a long time had passed, the Jews in Damascus conspired to kill" Saul. So the disciples of the Lord helped him escape from Damascus, in a basket lowered through an opening in the city wall (Acts 9:25).

He fled to Jerusalem. But even there, he was not welcomed. Everyone suspected his sudden conversion, until Barnabas came to his defense. Barnabas was a Hellenistic Jew from the island of Cyprus, near Tarsus. He brought Saul to the apostles (probably only Peter and James), told of his conversion, and his zeal for the faith in Damascus. Saul then went about freely, speaking boldly in the name of the Lord and debating with the Hellenists, his former buddies. When they conspired to kill him, the disciples of the Lord sent him to Caesarea and then back to Tarsus.

Saul stayed at Tarsus four or five years (c. 40-44 A.D.), leading a hidden life, as Jesus once had. Around 44 A.D., Barnabas went to Tarsus and brought Saul to work at Antioch (Acts 11:25-26).

Thus Luke proved conclusively that Saul had a right to be reckoned as one of the Twelve. He was called by and saw the risen and glorified Christ; he was to suffer like the apostles (Acts 5:41); and he was filled with the Holy Spirit, just as they were at Pentecost.

Life is made up of alternations of storm and calm, persecution and peace. Peace came to the Church now, because its chief persecutor had been converted and because the Jews were preoccupied with Caligula who wanted to set up his image in the Holy of Holies in the Temple. After peace had settled in the Church, it grew in numbers. While the deacons were active, the apostles were not inactive. Luke demonstrates the actions of Peter to show how truly he succeeded Jesus.

Preparing the Church for the Gentiles. To confirm the work of Philip, Peter in the year 39 A.D. visited the cities he had evangelized: Lydda, Joppa, and Caesarea.

This tour of Peter sets the final act in the preparation of the Church for its worldwide mission: the conversion of Cornelius and his reception into the Church by Peter.

Peter went first to the holy ones living in Lydda. (Enemies called the Church "the Way"; believers liked to call themselves "saints" or "holy ones"—those set apart.) Lydda was a day's journey, about 23 miles to the northwest of Jerusalem. There, Peter healed a man named Aeneas who had been confined to bed for eight years, for he was paralyzed. Peter, like Jesus curing the paralytic, used practically the same words: "Get up and make your bed." As a result of the miracle, "All the inhabitants of Lydda turned to the Lord."

News spread to Joppa, nine miles away. A disciple of the Lord, Tabitha (in Aramaic) or Dorcas (in Greek) had died. She had been renowned for her great deeds of charity. So two men were sent to Lydda to ask Peter to come to Joppa. When he arrived there, the situation was much like that when Jesus arrived at the house of Jairus, whose daughter had just died. The parallel is unmistakable. Jesus put out the mourners and said, "Talitha, cumi" ("damsel, arise"). Peter did the same: he put out the mourners and said, "Tabitha, rise up." The one difference, however, was that Jesus cured by His own power; Peter cured in the name of Jesus. Yet Luke's message is clear: Peter is the vicar of Christ—he takes Christ's place as the head of the apostles and in working miracles.

The resurrection of Tabitha opened the door to Peter's work in Joppa, an important seaport town. Peter resolved to stay there for a while and took up lodgings with one Simon, a tanner. This was significant for both Jewish and Gentile Christians, for the tanning occupation was considered unclean. Rabbis said, "It is impossible to do without tanners, but woe to the man who is a tanner." Jews forbade tanners to dwell in towns, thus Simon's place in Joppa was by the seashore. Peter showed that he had made great strides in overcoming Jewish exclusivism by choosing to reside at a tanner's home.

The Vision of Cornelius (10:1-8). By far the most important event on Peter's missionary journey was the conversion of Cornelius. There is a progression: at Lydda, Peter healed sickness; at Joppa, he raised the dead; but at Caesarea, he brought the gospel to the Gentile world. The fact that Luke devotes nearly two chapters to this story indicates that he recognized it as one of the most important events in the history of the Church. Luke presents it as a drama in four acts.

Act 1: Caesarea. Caesarea was 38 miles north of Joppa. It was built by Herod the Great in honor of Augustus Caesar (22 B.C.) on the Mediterranean. Caesarea in Galilee was called Caesarea-Philippi to distinguish it from Caesarea on the Mediterranean. This latter Caesarea was the seat of the Roman government in Palestine. Hence a Roman garrison was there.

Among the soldiers stationed there was Cornelius, a centurion belonging to the Italian Cohort. His family had given great men to Rome, like Sulla and the Scipios. He himself was a God-fearing man; one of the many pagans who had adopted Jewish monotheism, its lofty ethics, its Scripture, and synagogue worship. However, he had not submitted to circumcision or Jewish dietary laws and so he was still considered a Gentile.

Though Cornelius was a religious man, it was not enough: he needed the gospel. True religion comes by means of the principle of exhaustion; that is, if one does his best, God will do the rest; if one uses an imperfect form of religion and lives it sincerely and faithfully, God will lead such a one out of it into something better. Judaism can lead to Christianity; but Judaism alone is not enough. Therefore, an angel of God came to Cornelius and told him to send messengers to Joppa to summon Peter to his home. Cornelius sent two servants and a devout soldier.

Act 2: Joppa, Peter's Vision. Again, God works at both ends of the line, as with Philip and the eunuch, Saul and Ananias. He prepared Cornelius at Caesarea and Peter at Joppa. What a confirmation this incident was of Peter's leadership. Philip, the evangelist of Samaria, lived in Caesarea, a few moments away from

Cornelius. Yet God called Peter over 38 miles away to receive him into the Church, for this was a monumental breakthrough in the spread of the gospel and so needed the sanction of the head of the Church.

While Peter was at prayer at noontime, he received a vision. He saw a big sheet or sail, perhaps suggested by the sails in the harbor. Clean and unclean animals were in it. Was Peter bothered in being in the home of a tanner, one unclean? Was he praying for light on the matter? It could be.

A praying Gentile is the first uncircumcised person to enter the Church; and a praying apostle is the first to instruct him. It is good to have fixed times for prayers, as did the Jews. Forms can lead to formalism, but fixed times of prayer can prevent spiritual decay and sloth.

Since it was noontime, Peter was hungry; so a voice ordered him to eat of the unclean animals, lowered in the sheet. Peter refused. The heavenly voice said, "What God has made clean, you are not to call profane." The distinction between clean and unclean in Judaism was as clear to a Jew as the distinction of colors is to us. It was so rooted in the Jewish mentality that only a creative act of God Himself could have done away with this tradition.

The meaning of the vision was that henceforth there is nothing in Christianity that is unclean. Peter is not to fear to socialize with the Gentiles.

The great sheet tied at the four corners symbolized the earth. The clean and unclean animals, the entire human race: Jews and Gentiles. The sheet being lowered from heaven signified that all people come from God. The command to kill and eat the unclean animals implied that discrimination is to be put to death, no longer to be made between people. The command was given three times to indicate how deeply rooted this dietary tradition was in the minds and hearts of the people.

Even after such a revelation, because of habit and training, Peter still had his doubts. So what does he do? He takes six others of his brothers with him when he goes to Cornelius. Misery loves company.

Act 3: Caesarea—Peter and Cornelius meet. What faith the centurion had! He calculated just how long it would take Peter and the others to return. At the estimated time, he had all his kinsmen and friends there to meet them.

We might ask, "Why become a Catholic?" Cornelius was a very good man. He had so much to commend him. What need had he of the gospel?

Religion is not just a system of ethics: of do's and don'ts. Religion is Christ. Cornelius lacked Christ. And Christ is the way to the Father. Without Christ, one cannot really know God nor truly love Him.

Philosophy and Reason alone are not enough to raise man above this world. Our destiny is SUPER-natural. Cornelius, though good, needed Christ and the Holy Spirit.

Peter's Speech (10:34-43). Peter starts off with an observation that is a revelation to him. "I see," he said, "that God is no respecter of persons. I and the other Jews thought He was, for we were His chosen people. I see now that a good man, no matter his nationality, is acceptable to Him."

A second point needed clarification: Jesus had been accused of high treason and crucified as King of the Jews. This must have attracted the attention of the military. In the mind of a Roman officer, there must have lurked the suspicion that one whom the Roman Governor had sentenced to death must in some way have been guilty. Certainly Cornelius, who would never have stooped to an unjust act, would have found it difficult to believe that an officer, so highly placed as Pilate, would ever stoop so low as to condemn an innocent man.

So Peter affirmed the innocence of Jesus. He pointed out that this Jesus was no revolutionary agitator, but a preacher of peace and a doer of good works. Then, in parenthesis, He dropped a bombshell by asserting that this same Jesus is the Lord of all—not, like Caesar, Lord of only an Empire.

Finally, Peter launched into the life of Jesus. After His baptism by John, Peter said, Jesus went about doing good: casting out demons and healing the sick. Yet the Jews put Him to death by hanging Him on a tree. But God raised Him up from the dead on the third day to prove His innocence. We were witnesses of all this.

Then he went on to tell how Jesus had commissioned them to preach Him to all nations—to preach how He would be the judge of the living and the dead, a fact attested to by the prophets; to preach that before His coming as judge, He comes as Savior: granting the forgiveness of sins to all who believe in Him.

What delicacy and tact Peter used in this sermon. No mention was made of Pontius Pilate, nor of Roman crucifixion. Peter used instead the Hebrew phrase: "hanging him on a tree." A first reading of this account would lead one to think that only the Jews and those who dwelt around Jerusalem had anything to do with the death of Jesus.

When the resurrection is mentioned, Peter used no quotes from Scripture as he did for his Jewish audience on Pentecost. Instead, he used common sense arguments: "We ate and drank with him after he rose from the dead."

Peter's sermon was like the gospel; a record of facts; out of the facts grew the doctrines; and out of the doctrines emerged the morals. Peter did not say, "Do this and don't do that." His sermon was not a lesson in morality.

It was an account of a Person who, although himself a man, had changed and reversed the condition of man; had broken the power of sin and Satan so many times as to show he could do it in all and for all; had lived a life such as no other man had ever lived; had spoken such as never man spoke; then gave His life to save all; after dying He rose to be mediator with God for all who believe and to be the judge of all those will not believe.

In a word, Peter's sermon was our Apostle's Creed on Jesus. It is really the outline Mark used in his gospel. Mark's gospel has often been described as an expansion of this sermon of Peter's. For this reason Peter's sermon is one of the most important examples of apostolic preaching in Acts—the Kerygma.

The Baptism of Cornelius (10:44-49). Such a preacher— Peter, a man of prayer and the Spirit; and such an audience— Cornelius and his household, prayerful and eager; could have but one effect; a new Pentecost. "While Peter was still speaking these things, the Holy Spirit fell upon all who were listening to the word."

A preacher once asked the great actor Garrick, "How is it you can so easily raise the feelings of your audiences by dramatizing fiction and I cannot move my people by preaching the truth?"

Garrick answered, "Because I recite falsehoods as if they were true, whereas you preach truths as if they were fiction."

The Spirit came while Peter spoke. But even with the Spirit, baptism is necessary. So Peter ordered Cornelius and his household to be baptized in the name of Jesus Christ.

Act 4: Jerusalem (11:1-18). The reaction of the Jerusalem Church to Peter's baptism of Cornelius was not one of rejoicing but of criticism. "You entered the house of the uncircumcised and ate with them." A great man, Peter, was criticized for a noble work. He was criticized for eating, not for preaching the gospel. The Christian Jews in Jerusalem still thought like Jews. Conversion is ever so slow a process: first the blade, the ear, then the full corn.

Peter's defense settled once and for all the fundamental issue of whether Christians must live as Jews under the law of Moses. Thus he prepared the Church in Jerusalem for the great climactic act in the Acts; namely, the evangelization of the Greeks and the founding of the Church at Antioch.

Acts 11:19-12:25

Ch 11.

The Church at Antioch [19] Now those who had been scattered by the persecution that arose because of Stephen went as far as Phoenicia, Cyprus, and Antioch, preaching the word to no one but Jews. [20] There were some Cypriots and Cyrenians among them, however, who came to Antioch and began to speak to the Greeks as well, proclaiming the Lord Jesus. [21] The hand of the Lord was with them and a great number who believed turned to the Lord. [22] The news about them reached the ears of the church in Jerusalem, and they sent Barnabas [to of] to Antioch. [23] When he arrived and saw the grace of God, he rejoiced and encouraged them all to remain faithful to the Lord in firmness of heart, [24] for he was a good man, filled with the Holy Spirit and faith. And a large number of people was added to the Lord. [25] Then he went to Tarsus to look for Saul, [26] and when he had found him he brought him to Antioch. For a whole year they met with the church and taught a large number of people, and it was in Antioch that the disciples were first called Christians.

The Prediction of Agabus [27] At that time some prophets came down from Jerusalem to Antioch, [28] and one of them named Agabus stood up and predicted by the Spirit that there would be a sever famine all over the world, and it happened under Claudius. [29] So the disciples determined that, according to ability, each should send relief to the brothers who lived in Judea. [30] This they did, sending it to the presbyters in care of Barnabas and Saul.

12 Herod's Persecution of the Christians [1] About that time King Herod laid hands upon some members of the church to harm them. [2] He had James, the brother of John, killed by the sword, [3] and when he saw that this was pleasing to the Jews he proceeded to arrest Peter also. (It was [the]feast of Unleavened Bread.) [4] He had him taken into custody and put in prison under the guard of four squads of four soldiers each. He intended to bring him before the people after Passover. [5] Peter thus was being kept in prison, but prayer by the church was fervently being made to God on his behalf.

[6] On the very night before Herod was to bring him to trial, Peter, secured by double chains, was sleeping between two soldiers, while outside the door guards kept watch on the prison. [7] Suddenly the angel of the Lord stood by him and a light shone in the cell. He tapped Peter on the side and awakened him, saying, "Get up quickly." The chains fell from his wrists. [8] The angel said to him, "Put on your belt and your sandals." He did so. Then he said to him, "Put on your cloak and follow me." [9] So he followed him out, not realizing that what was happening through the angel was real; he thought he was seeing a vision. [10] They passed the first guard, then the second, and came to the iron gate leading out to the city, which opened for them by itself. They emerged and made their way down an alley, and suddenly the angel left him. [11] Then Peter recovered his senses and said, " Now I know for certain that [the] Lord sent his angel and rescued me from the hand of Herod and from all that the Jewish people had been expecting." [12] When he realized this, he went to the house of Mary, the mother of John who is called Mark, where there were many people gathered in prayer. [13] When he knocked on the gateway door, a maid named Rhoda came to answer it. [14] She was so overjoyed when she recognized Peter's voice that, instead of opening the gate, she ran in and announced that Peter was standing at the gate. [15] They told her, "You are out of your mind," but she insisted that it was so. But they kept saying, "It is his angel." [16] But Peter continued to knock, and when they opened it, they saw him and were astounded. [17] He motioned to them with his hand to be quiet and explained [to them] how the Lord had led him out of the prison, and said, "Report this to James and the brothers." Then he left and went to another place. [18] At daybreak there was no small commotion among the soldiers over what had become of Peter. [19] Herod, after instituting a search but not finding him, ordered the guards tried and executed. Then he left Judea to spend some time in Caesarea.

Herod's Death [20] He had long been very angry with the people of Tyre and Sidon, who now came to him in a body. After winning over Blastus, the king's chamberlain, *they sued for peace because* their country was supplied with food from the king's territory. [21] On an appointed day, Herod, attired in royal robes, [and] seated on the rostrum, addressed them publicly. [22] The assembled crowd cried out, "This is the voice of a god, not of a man." [23] At once the angel of the Lord struck him down because he did not ascribe the honor to God, and he was eaten by worms and breathed his last. [24] But the word of God continued to spread and grow.

Mission of Barnabas and Saul [25] After Barnabas and Saul completed their relief mission, they returned to Jerusalem, taking with them John, who is called Mark.

Facts on Acts

CHAPTER 9

Expansion of the Church

The Church at Antioch (11:19-30). Some of the refugees from Jerusalem, dispersed after Stephen's death, had gone to Antioch; but there, they preached to Jews only. However, some of the Hellenistic Jews from Cyprus and Cyrene, began to preach to the Greeks there. Peter's reception of Cornelius served to escalate this trend.

The Church developed in three stages. In the first stage, from its establishment on Sinai down to the Babylonian Captivity, it was strictly Jewish.

The second stage happened after the Captivity. During the Captivity, some of the Jews became liberals and broadminded because of their enforced association with the Gentiles; therefore on their return to Jerusalem after the Captivity, they built a Court of the Gentiles in their Temple—a thing Solomon never ever dreamt of doing. From then on the Jews sought proselytes. Though they did not pull down the wall separating Jew and Gentile, they did put a few gates in it through which the Gentiles could pass into Judaism.

The third stage came about in Antioch. There, the wall of separation between Jew and Gentile was pulled down, and Greeks were made Christians without first having to become Jews. It was a whole new church; and its members were given the name "Christians" (probably by the Roman authorities, for the word derives from the Latin)—a name that showed them as totally distinct from Judaism.

These Greeks received the gospel enthusiastically. Again, the Church in Jerusalem was concerned, but not alarmed. She sent—

kindly enough—not a Palestinian Jewish Christian, but a Cypriot, Barnabas, to investigate. Barnabas was a gracious man, kind and encouraging. His name meant "son of consolation or exhortation."

The moment he saw the community at Antioch, he knew that the Spirit had been at work there. Everyone there was so Christlike that they deserved to be called "Christians." So he joined them, consoled them, exhorted them to remain faithful to the Lord. As a result a large number of people were added to the Lord.

Barnabas saw, however, that more was needed than exhortation in the church at Antioch. A great teacher was needed. A flower has beauty and aroma, a man has a head and a heart. Barnabas could touch the heart, but he felt he could not touch the head. He felt he was no teacher. The best teacher he knew was Saul of Tarsus. The Church today calls Paul "the teacher of the world" (Preface for Feasts of Sts. Peter and Paul, June 29). So Barnabas went to Tarsus and brought Saul back to Antioch. They worked together there for a whole year, and the people grew in numbers, grace and knowledge.

The Antiochene Community. Antioch in Syria is to be distinguished from Antioch in Pisidia. Syrian Antioch was the third largest city in the Empire—Rome and Alexandria alone were larger.

It is significant that the brethren were not called Christian in Jerusalem, for there they were looked upon merely as a pious sect within Judaism. Except for their belief in the divinity of Jesus and in the presence of the Holy Spirit, they seemed no different from the rest of their countrymen. For them public liturgy meant participation in the Temple services, where they still went to pray publicly. Privately, however, they broke bread in their homes. They had their foot in the world of the Old Testament and one in that of the New.

But at Antioch, due to the distance from the Temple, a number of new characteristics emerged in the Christian community there. First, the majority in the community consisted of pagan converts, who had been received into the Church without having had to go through Judaism.

Secondly, because the Temple was so far away, the breaking of the bread became the public liturgy of the community (13:2).

Thirdly, at such a liturgy the real missionary spirit of the Church manifested itself. "While they were worshipping the Lord (*leitourgounton*="making liturgy to the Lord") and fasting, the Holy Spirit said, 'Set apart for me Barnabas and Saul for the work to which I have called them'" (13:2). This work meant preaching the gospel not only to the Jews of the dispersion but also to the pagans of Asia Minor. This call, as we shall see, inaugurated Paul's First Missionary Journey.

And so, at Antioch, there was an integrated community, mostly Greek converts, where the Eucharist was the center of public worship, where the missionary spirit manifested itself, and where the disciples of the Lord were first called Christians..

Antioch was a beautiful city on the Orontes. It was rich, the crossroads between the East and the West; pleasure-loving; more wicked than Rome. When the Antiochenes saw men and women, who just admired beauty, were detached from wealth, spurned the sinful pleasures of the city, they asked, "Who taught you this? Who gave you these new ideas about beauty, wealth, pleasure and sin (as you call it)?"

They always answered, "Christ. He taught us about a world and a beauty that would never pass away. He taught us to beware of the pleasures that lead to sin. He taught us not to worship your gods."

So they would say, "He then is your God?"

And they would answer, "Yes."

Some scoffed at them and called them names, like "Christ men"—one who followed a crucified god. Others, however, admired them and saw in the name a label that perfectly described those who could do nothing but talk about their Christ and become like Him. Since the name "Christian" arrowed in to the core of Christianity, Christ, it stuck.

The Prediction of Agabus (11:27-30). Some prophets came down from Jerusalem and one of them, Agabus, predicted there would be a severe famine in the reign of Claudius (41-54 A.D.). When the famine came in 46-48 A.D., the Christians of Antioch showed the genuiness of their faith by sending relief to the brothers in Jerusalem through Saul and Barnabas, who turned over the fund to the presbyters, the elders in Jerusalem. What power Christianity has to unite opposites: here we have Gentiles helping Jews!

Herod's Persecution of the Christians (12:1-19). Herod Agrippa I was the cousin of Herod Antipas who ruled Galilee from 4 B.C. to 37 A.D.—that fox who beheaded John the Baptist, mocked Christ, built Tiberias. Caligula exiled him in 37 A.D. and turned over Galilee to Agrippa in 39 A.D. Then when Caligula was assassinated in 41 A.D., his successor Claudia made Agrippa King of Samaria and Judea.

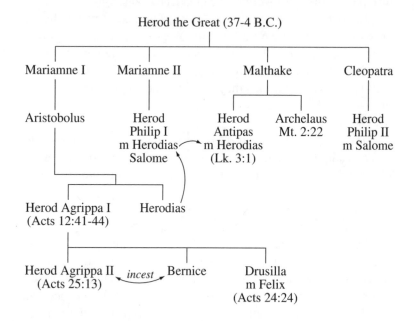

By restoring the kingship of Herod, Roman power was removed. With its removal went Roman justice. Christians could expect the worst. The Pharisees hated them. Even the Jewish people were turning against them, because they were receiving Gentiles without imposing the law of Moses on them. So the apostles decided to leave Jerusalem. James the Just would remain to lead the small community left there.[1]

SPAIN - 3

BRITAIN 10

SCYTHIA - 4

ROME - 1

PATRAS 4 — ACHAIA 4

PATIMOS - 2

BITHYNIA - 4 - 7
ASIA MINOR - 2   GALATIA - 4
PHRYGIA - 5   CAPPADOCIA - 4
EPHESUS - 2
• ANTIOCH - 1
PHOENICIA - 11
• JERUSALEM - 9
JUDEA - 12

SYRIA - 11

PARTHIA - 6
ARMENIA - 7 - 8
INDIA - 6 - 7

MESOPOTAMIA - 10

PERSIA 6 - 7

EGYPT - 10
NORTH AFRICA - 10

ARABIA - 7 - 8 - 9

1 - PETER / 2 - JOHN / 3 JAMES THE GREATER
4 - ANDREW / 5 - PHILIP / 6 - THOMAS
7 - BARTHOLOMEW / 8 - MATTHEW
9 - JAMES THE LESSER / 10 - SIMON THE ZEALOT
11 - JUDE THADDEUS / 12 - MATTHIAS

DISPERSION OF THE TWELVE APOSTLES AND PROPAGATION OF THE BIBLE
According to the sacred text or multi-century tradition

(C. Bernard Fuffin, *The Twelve*, Our Sunday Visitor, Indianna)

Their fears were well-founded, for very soon after coming to Judea, Herod, to win the favor of both priests and people, beheaded James, the son of Zebedee in the spring of 42 A.D.

When Herod saw how pleasing this was to the Jews, he arrested Peter. He kept Peter in prison under 16 guards, intending to

---

[1]   Tradition places the dispersion of the apostles on July 15, 42 A.D.

Andrew went to Scythia and perhaps Greece.

Bartholomew to south Arabia, perhaps India.

Jude Thaddaeus to Syria.

Matthew to Armenia and/or Ethiopia.

Matthias entirely unknown.

Philip to Asia Minor.

Simon the Zealous to Mesopotamia.

Thomas to Parthia and India.

The most striking fact about this is that these apostles went beyond the boundaries of the Roman Empire. The truth is that they believed Christ meant what He said when He told His disciples to carry the gospel to the ends of the earth.

Another interesting fact is that it is very probable that at this time St. Matthew wrote his gospel in Aramaic for the faithful in Judea, and in Greek for the Jews of the Dispersion. He did this with the help of the other apostles. Also at this time, John probably took Mary to Ephesus where they stayed until the death of Agrippa in 44 A.D.

try him before the people after the Passover celebration. "But prayer by the Church was fervently being made to God on his behalf." The early Church realized the importance of Peter. So it used its only weapon: prayer; and prayer won out.

On the night before his trial, Peter slept—he had taken off his belt and sandals, he wanted a good sleep. And he got it. What a good conscience Peter had! What confidence in the Lord! He was sleeping soundly when the angel of the Lord came to release him from prison.

The angel freed him every so easily. Nothing is impossible with God.

Freed, Peter went to the house of Mary, sister of Barnabas and mother of John Mark. Mary was well-to-do. Her home was big enough for a prayer meeting. When Peter knocked at the door, Rhoda (Rose) answered it. When she recognized Peter's voice, she was so overjoyed, she left him standing there and raced back to tell the others.

How strange was their reaction: they had been praying fervently for this and could not believe it when their prayers were answered. They said to Rhoda, "You're out of your mind." She insisted. They said, "It is his angel." (You see Christians believed from the very beginning in the doctrine of the guardian angels.)

Peter kept knocking and was finally let in. All were astounded. Peter explained what the Lord had done and told them to "report this to James and the brothers." This James was not the son of Zebedee, whom Herod had beheaded. This James (little Jim) was "the brother of the Lord" —Jesus' cousin, son of Alphaeus and Mary. Then Peter "left and went to another place."[2] Herod's perse-

---

[2]   Peter planned to go to Rome. He went by way of Antioch and Asia Minor and arrived at Rome near the end of 42 A.D. The following year Peter seems to have made his first notable convert, Pomponia Graecina, wife of Aulus Plautius, commander of the Roman armies in Britian. Sienkiewicz in his novel *Quo Vadis* has this Plautius crucified in the arena under Nero as a Christian.

Peter stayed seven years in Rome until Claudius expelled the Jews from Rome in 49 A.D., because of disturbances, according to the pagan historian Suetonius, caused by the Jews and followers of Simon Magus over one called "Chrestus" (the Latin for the Greek *Christos).*

Peter returned to Jerusalem for the death of Mary in the year 49 and the Council of Jerusalem in the year 50.

cution closes this transitional period of the Church from being localized to becoming universal.

The next day there was a big commotion over the escape of Peter from prison. Rage must have its victims, so cruel Herod executed the guards. Then he left Judea, in disgust and anger at Peter's escape. He went to Caesarea.

There, ambassadors came to Herod from the seaport towns of Tyre and Sidon. For some reason or other, Herod had long been angry with the Tyrians and Sidonians. We do not know why. But we know that Tyre and Sidon, being seaport towns, were dependent upon Herod's realm for both trade and food. War would have been tragic for the seacoast cities. So they sent ambassadors to Herod at Caesarea in a most submissive manner. Bribing Blastus, Herod's chamberlin, a hearing was obtained for them with Herod. In his vanity, Herod determined to receive these ambassadors with a display of royal splendor.

In the year 44 A.D., games were held to celebrate the Emperor Claudius' safe return to Rome from Britain. So, Herod came into the theater, erected by his grandfather, robed in silver garments. The morning sun made him glow in light, so that some said it was a divine apparition. After he had delivered an eloquent oration, the people shouted, "This is the voice of a god, not a man." Herod gloried in this idolatry. So God struck him down, as He had other persecutors (2 Mac. 9:9). He was carried from the theater, stricken with a searing pain in his bowels. After five days of painful agony, he succumbed to a gruesome death, "eaten by worms."

When a Roman emperor went out upon some grand day in all his imperial pomp, an officer would go before him to burn flax and cry out, *Sic transit gloria mundi*— so passes the glory of the world: it vanishes like the smoke from the burnt flax. So Herod was gone, like a whiff of smoke in the air; but the Church he despised and persecuted "continued to spread and grow." Why? Because of the gifts of the Spirit, the zeal of the apostles, the divine power attendant upon the word, the example of the first Christians, the judgment of God on the persecutors, and the united prayers of the Church.

Paul and Barnabas had probably witnessed all that Herod had done in Jerusalem, for they were in the city with relief funds. When they left for Antioch, John Mark, the nephew of Barnabas, went with them.

The stage was now set for the extension of the Church—the First Missionary Journey of St. Paul (c. 45 A.D.)

Acts 13:1-52

13 [1] Now there were in the church at Antioch prophets and teachers: Barnabas, Symeon who was called Niger, Lucius of Cyrene, Manaen who was a close friend of Herod the tetrarch, and Saul. [2] While there were worshipping the Lord and fasting, the Holy Spirit said, "Set apart for me Barnabas and Saul for the work to which I have called them." [3] Then, completing their fasting and prayer, they laid hands on them and sent them off.

First Mission Begins in Cyprus [4] So they, sent forth by the Holy Spirit, went down to Seleucia and from there sailed to Cyprus. [5] When they arrived in Salamis, they proclaimed the word of God in the Jewish synagogues. They had John also as their assistant. [6] When they had traveled through the whole island as far as Paphos, they met a magician named Bar-Jesus who was a Jewish false prophet. [7] He was with the proconsul Sergius Paulus, a man of intelligence, who had summoned Barnabas and Saul and wanted to hear the word of God. [8] But Elymas the magician (for that is what his names means) opposed them in an attempt to turn the proconsul away from the faith. [9] But Saul, also known as Paul, filled with the Holy Spirit, looked intently at him [10] and said, "You son of the devil, you enemy of all that is right, full of every sort of deceit and fraud. Will you not stop twisting the straight paths of [the] Lord? [11] Even now the hand of the Lord is upon you. You will be blind, and unable to see the sun for a time" Immediately a dark mist fell upon him, and he went about seeking people to lead him by the hand, [12] When the proconsul saw what had happened, he came to believe, for he was astonished by the teaching about the Lord.

Paul's Arrival at Antioch in Pisidia [13] From Paphos, Paul and his companions set sail and arrived at Perga in Pamphylia. But John left them and returned to Jerusalem. [14] They continued on from Perga and reached Antioch in Pisidia. On the sabbath they entered [into] the synagogue and took their seats. [15] After the reading of the law and the prophets, the synagogue officials sent word to them, "My brothers, if one of you has a word of exhortation for the people, please speak."

Paul's Address in the Synagogue [16] So Paul got up, motioned with his hand, and said, "Fellow Israelites and you others who are God-fearing, listen. [17] The God of this people Israel chose our ancestors and exalted the people during their sojourn in the land of Egypt. With uplifted arms he led them out of it [18] and for about forty years he put up with them in the desert. [19] When he had destroyed seven nations in the land of Canaan, he gave them their land as an inheritance [20] at the end of about four hundred and fifty years. After these things he provided judges up to Samuel [the] prophet. [21] Then they asked for a king. God gave them Saul, son of Kish, a man from the tribe of Benjamin, for forty years. [22] Then he removed him and raised up David as their king; of him he testified, 'I have found David, son of Jesse, a man after my own heart; he will carry out my every wish.' [23] From this man's descendants God, according to his promise, has brought to Israel a savior, Jesus. [24] John heralded his coming by proclaiming a baptism of repentance to all the people of Israel; [25] and as John was completing his course, he would say, 'What do you suppose that I am? I am not he. Behold, one is coming after me; I am not worthy to unfasten the sandals on his feet'

[26] "My brothers, children of the family of Abraham, and those others among you who are God-fearing, to us this word of salvation has been sent. [27] The inhabitants of Jerusalem and their leaders failed to recognize him, and by condemning him they fulfilled the oracles of the prophets that are read sabbath after sabbath. [28] For even though they found no grounds for a death sentence, they asked Pilate to have him put to death, [29] and when they had accomplished all that was written about him, they took him down from the tree and placed him in a tomb. [30] But God raised him from the dead, [31] and for many days he appeared to those who had come up with him from Galilee to Jerusalem. These are [now] his witnesses before the people. [32] We ourselves are proclaim-

ing this good news to you that what God promised our ancestors [33] he has brought to fulfillment for us, [their] children, by raising up Jesus, as it is written in the second psalm. 'You are my son; this day I have begotten you.' [34] And that he raised him from the dead never to return to corruption he declared in this way, 'I shall give you the benefits assured to David.' [35] That is why he also says in another psalm, 'You will not suffer your holy one to see corruption.'

[36] Now David, after he had served the will of God in his lifetime, fell asleep, was gathered to his ancestors, and did see corruption. [37] But the one whom God raised up did not see corruption. [38] You must know, my brothers, that through him forgiveness of sins is being proclaimed to you, [and] in regard to everything from which you could not be justified under the law of Moses, [39] in him every believer is justified. [40] Be careful, then, that what was said in the prophets not come about:

[41] 'Look on, you scoffers,
    be amazed and disappear.
For I am doing a work in your days,
    a work that you will never believe even if
      someone tells you.'"

[42] As they were leaving, they invited them to speak on these subjects the following Sabbath. [43] After the congregation had dispersed, any Jews and worshippers who were converts to Judaism followed Paul and Barnabas, who spoke to them and urged them to remain faithful to the grace of God.

Address to the Gentiles [44] On the following sabbath almost the whole city gathered to hear the word of the Lord. [45] When the Jews saw the crowds, they were filled with jealousy and with violent abuse contradicted what Paul said. [46] Both Paul and Barnabas spoke out boldly and said, "It was necessary that the word of God be spoken to you first, but since you reject it and condemn yourselves as unworthy of eternal life, we now turn to the Gentiles. [47] For so the Lord has commanded us, 'I have made you a light to the

Gentiles, that you may be an instrument of salvation to the ends of the earth,'"

48 The Gentiles were delighted when they heard this and glorified the word of the Lord. All who were destined for eternal life came to believe, 49 and the word of the Lord continued to spread through the whole regions. 50 The Jews, *however, incited the women of* prominence who were worshipers and the leading men of the city, stirred up a persecution against Paul and Barnabas, and expelled them from their territory. 51 So they shook the dust from their feet in protest against them and went to Iconium. 52 The disciples were filled with joy and the Holy Spirit.

Acts **14:1-28**

14 Paul and Barnabas at Iconium. 1 In Iconium they entered the Jewish synagogue together and spoke in such a way that a great number of both Jews and Greeks came to believe, 2 although the disbelieving Jews stirred up and poisoned the minds of the Gentiles against the brothers. 3 So they stayed for a considerable period, speaking out boldly for the Lord, who confirmed the word about his grace by granting signs and wonders to occur through their hands. 4 The people of the city were divided: some were with the Jews; others, with the apostles. 5 When there was an attempt by both the Gentiles and the Jews, together with their leaders, to attack and stone them, 6 they realized it and fled to the Lycaonian cities of Lystra and Derbe and to the surrounding countryside, 7 where they continued to proclaim the good news.

Paul and Barnabas at Lystra 8 At Lystra there was a crippled man, lame from birth, who had never walked. 9 He listened to Paul speaking, who looked intently at him, saw that he had the faith to be healed, 10 and called out in a loud voice, "Stand up straight on your feet." He jumped up and began to walk about. 11 When the crowds saw what Paul had done, they cried out in Lycaonian, "The gods have come down to us in human form." [12] They called Barnabas "Zeus" and Paul "Hermes," because he was the chief speaker. [13] And the priest of Zeus, whose temple was at the entrance to the city, brought oxen and garlands to the gates, for he together with the people intended to offer sacrifice.

[14] The apostles Barnabas and Paul tore their garments when they heard this and rushed out into the crowd, shouting, [15] "Men, why are you doing this? We are of the same nature as you, human beings. We proclaim to you good news that you should turn from these idols to the living God, 'who made heaven and earth and sea and all that is in them.' [16] In past generations he allowed all Gentiles to go their own ways; [17] yet, in bestowing his goodness, he did not leave himself without witness, for he gave you rains from heaven and fruitful seasons, and filled you with nourishment and gladness for your hearts." [18] Even with these words, they scarcely restrained the crowds from offering sacrifice to them.

[19] However, some Jews from Antioch and Iconium arrived and won over the crowds. They stoned Paul and dragged him out of the city, supposing that he was dead. [20] But when the disciples gathered around him, he got up and entered the city. On the following day he left with Barnabas for Derbe.

End of the First Mission [21] After they had proclaimed the good news to that city and made a considerable number of disciples, they returned to Lystra and to Iconium and to Antioch. [22] They strengthened the spirits of the disciples and exhorted them to persevere in the faith, saying, "It is necessary for us to undergo many hardships to enter the kingdom of God." [23] They appointed presbyters for them in each church and, with prayer and fasting, commended them to the Lord in whom they had put their faith. [24] Then they traveled through Pisidia and reached Pamphylia. [25] After proclaiming the word at Perga they went down to Attalia. [26] From there they sailed to Antioch, where they had been commended to the grace of God for the work they had now accomplished. [27] And when they arrived, they called the church together and reported what God had done with them and how he had opened the door of faith to the Gentiles. [28] Then they spent no little time with the disciples.

CHAPTER 10

Paul's First Missionary
Journey 45 - 49 A.D.
1100 miles

(Acts 13-14)

Mission of Barnabas and Saul (13:1-3). Strong people make a congregation strong. "Now there were in the Church at Antioch prophets and teachers." The prophets were itinerant preachers, like Agabus (11:28), attached to no Church: they listened to the word of God then told it to their fellow Christians. The teachers were those who instructed persons won to the faith by the preaching of the apostles. They were the catechists of the early Church.

The list of the prophets and teachers at Antioch exemplify the universal appeal of the gospel. For instance, there was Paul from Tarsus, a trained rabbi; there was Joseph, called Barnabas, Son of Consolation, early defender of Paul and the brightest light in the community; there was Simon called by the African name Niger, the black (he could well have been Simon of Cyrene who helped Jesus carry His cross); Lucius could have been Simon's companion, for he also came from Cyrene, a North African settlement; Manaen was a man with courtly connections, he was a close friend of Herod Antipas, the tetrarch of Galilee.

It was the custom in those days to adopt a child as a companion for a young prince, thus forming what would seem a companionship for life. Manaen was brought up with Herod Antipas. He no doubt met John the Baptizer; maybe John converted Manaen.

Very likely, Manaen witnessed the mocking of Christ before Herod—perhaps that incident was what caused him to break with Herod. Luke might have gotten his information about Herod and the Baptist, and about the Baptist and Herodias, from Manaen.

As this strong community "were making liturgy to the Lord and fasting, the Holy Spirit said, 'Set apart for me Barnabas and Saul for the work to which I have called them.'" The Holy Spirit chose his ministers and designated what work they were to do. For every candle God lights, He has a candlestick: a work to do. Generally, God calls those to higher service, who have served well in lesser roles, as Saul and Barnabas had—they had evangelized for years now in Antioch. So the Spirit called them to a greater vocation to become missionaries.

The Spirit did not say, "I have set apart"; but "Set apart for me." He ordered the Church to commission Saul and Barnabas. God always works through His Church. So, when the community had completed their fasting and praying, they laid hands on Saud and Barnabas and sent them off. Thus the first missionary journey in the Church began with the authority of both the Holy Spirit and the Church.

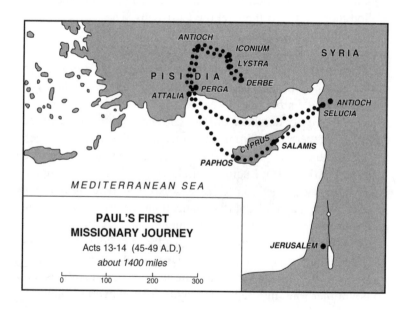

PAUL'S FIRST MISSIONARY JOURNEY
Acts 13-14 (45-49 A.D.)
about 1400 miles

First Mission Begins in Cyprus (13:4-12). These first foreign missionaries were Saul, Barnabas and John Mark. The three went 15 miles westward to the port of Antioch, Seleucia. For there, they sailed to Cyprus, Barnabas' homeland. Charity begins at home.

The Cyprians were mostly Greeks; even today four out of five are Greeks, the rest Turks. Cyprus was famous for its copper mines. The metal *cyprum* (copper) took its name from the island. The chief goddess of the island was Venus; the chief city of her worship was Paphos. There, Venus was worshipped by sacred prostitution (venereal acts); there, Satan had his seat.

Landing on the eastern side of the island of Cyprus, Saul and Barnabas went to the capital city, Salamis. Human sacrifice was practiced there. They proclaimed the works of God in the many Jewish synagogues in Salamis. John Mark was their assistant; that is, he probably did the baptizing. Peter didn't baptize Cornelius; and Paul said that he was sent, not to baptize, but to proclaim the good news. Their success must have been notable, for centuries later on of the bishops of Salamis was St. Epiphanius.

From Salamis, the trio headed straight across the island for Paphos, about sixty miles away, preaching all along the way. At Paphos the gospel encountered not only heathen vice in the dissolute worship of Venus but also heathen superstition in the person of a Jewish magician Bar-Jesus, who posed as a prophet.

At this time, impostors from the East, pretending to magical powers, had great influence over the Roman mind. The East, recently thrown open by Pompey's conquests, was land of mystery to the West. Reports of strange arts practiced there and of wonderful events that happened there excited, almost fanatically, the imagination of both the common people and the aristocracy of Rome. Even the strongest minds succumbed: Pompey, Crassus, Caesar sought the help of astrologers.

It is not strange, therefore, that Sergius Paulus, proconsul at Paphos, had Elymas as a confidential adviser. Paulus was a man of intelligence. He was groping for the truth. Elymas' Jewish theology was far better than paganism. yet it did not fully satisfy Paulus. So he summoned Barnabas and Saul to hear the word of God.

Elymas saw his position threatened, so he opposed the missionaries. It was then that the Holy Spirit came upon Saul, not

Barnabas. And Saul lashed out at Elymas. He called him, not Bar-Jesus, "son of Jesus," but Bar-Satan, "son of the devil." "you son of the devil," Paul thundered, "enemy of all that is right. You impostor and trickster, full of every deceit and fraud." Then to prove the truth of his words, Saul blinded him for a time. Instead of leading and guiding, Elymas now had to be led and guided. This blindness was but for a time, in the hopes that it might lead Elymas to the light of the truth. Sergius Paulus, having seen what had happened and astonished by the teaching about the Lord, came to believe.

From then on, Saul took over the leadership of the missionary band from Barnabas. The fact that the Holy Spirit had come upon Paul, instead of upon Barnabas, seemed to indicate that Paul was to be the chief leader in the evangelization of the Gentiles. Thus when they left Paphos, Luke writes: "Paul and his companions..."

When they had started out, Barnabas was the leader. Now it was Paul. What Caesarea Philippi was to Peter, Paphos was to Paul. It is tribute to the wonderful character of Barnabas that he did not complain nor resent the loss of position. If the change meant prospering the work of God, he was glad to take second place.

On this occasion also, Saul switched his name to Paul. Why the switch? In those days, most Jews had two names: a Jewish one, used among friends; and a Greek one, used in the wide world. Thus Cephas was Hebrew; and Peter, Greek. Saul was Hebrew; Paul was Greek. He used Paul now, because most probably it was in the best interest of his work as missionary to the Gentiles to use his Grecian name of Paul, which he had had from birth.

Paul's Arrival at Antioch in Pisidia (13:13-15). From Cyprus, Barnabas' homeland, the missionaries went to Perga in Pamphylia, Paul's homeland. John Mark left them there and returned to Jerusalem. Perhaps Mark resented Paul (not one of the twelve) taking over for his uncle Barnabas at Paphos. Maybe he couldn't swallow Paul's strong, anti-Judaic doctrine just yet. Mark was a friend of the fisherman, Peter; his heart was still at Jerusalem; his sympathies were Judaic; his natural friend and master was Peter, not Paul

Perhaps, too, Mark was timid; he was young. The savage aspect of Asia, the dangers of the Tuarian mountains, with peaks rising two miles high and with passes infested with robbers, with no prospects of food and shelter, could have frightened the lad. Many of Paul's perils that he speaks of in 2 Corinthians 11:26, from rivers, robbers and wilderness, could well have happened in this locality.

Or, most likely, Mark was just homesick. But whatever the reason, Paul was miffed and branded Mark a deserter. Yet God's ways are not man's. Had Mark not deserted, he might never have followed Peter, collected his memoirs, and written one of the earliest and most authentic of the Synoptics: once called Peter's Gospel, now known as the Gospel according to Mark.[1] Later on Mark and Paul were reconciled (Col. 4:10; 2 Timothy 4:11).

At Perga the stay was short. Perhaps Paul's health was bad at this time; so he sought the highlands. They climbed the Taurus Mountains, 3,600 feet above sea level. An in accordance with their missionary strategy, they focused on the large cities. So they forged ahead to Antioch in Pisidia, 100 miles to the north of Perga. There were 16 Antiochs in the Near East; two are mentioned in Acts: the Syrian Antioch that had sent out Barnabas and Saul; and the Pisidian Antioch to which they had now come.

Paul's Address in the Synagogue (13:16-43). The population of Antioch was a mixed one, having more Romans that usual in Asian cities, for it had been a Roman military colony. The Jews were probably a minority, for there is mention of only one synagogue in the city in contrast to the synagogues in Salamis.

As was their wont, they entered the synagogue on the Sabbath. Being strangers and devout, they were asked to speak.

So, Paul, not Barnabas, got up to speak. I suppose everybody was asking who these two were, so Paul motioned for quiet.

He began to win their good-will by calling them "fellow-Israelites"; then he addressed the God-fearers, Gentiles who had accepted Jewish monotheism. "Listen," he said; for the gospel calls for listening, since faith comes from hearing.

Life is made up of many experiences. We cannot tell the effect of any particular one. Many showers make the summer grass green. We cannot say exactly which one. So Paul's thoughts were formed

---

1 Mark's gospel was probably written during the three years (54-57 A.D.) he was with Peter in Rome.

by many experiences—apparently none impressed him so much as his contacts with Stephen and Peter.

Thus Paul's speech is divided into three parts. Each part begins with "Israelites" or "brothers" (verses 16, 26, 38). The first part echoes Stephen's speech' the second, Peter's at Pentecost; and third reflects Paul himself as seen in his later epistles.

Part 1 (16-25). Like Stephen, Paul began with a narrative of Jewish history. "God," he said, "chose our ancestors..." the implication was, that pagans have a chance, for God's choice was a free one, not based on any merits of Israel. Then he skimmed over the Egyptian and the desert experiences, the conquest of Canaan, Judges, Samuel, Kings (of course his namesake, Saul). But he zeroed in on David from whose descendants God promised to send a savior, Jesus. John heralded His coming.

The point Paul wanted to make here was the same point Stephen had made before his martyrdom; namely, that Jesus was the climax of Jewish history. For the pagan, history was cyclic: it went nowhere, around in circles. For the Christian, history is linear: it goes somewhere, toward the Parousia. Jewish history, too, was linear: it pointed to and reached its culmination in Jesus Christ.

Part 2 (26-37). Next, Paul parroted Peter. He told the Antiochene Jews and God-fearers that "the word of salvation" had come in Jesus; but the Jews had rejected Him and their leaders crucified Him according to the Scriptures. However, God is unconquerable, so Jesus arose from the dead. This is the glad tidings I announce: His resurrection according to the Scriptures. Then Paul argued for the resurrection of Jesus, exactly as Peter had at Pentecost, by quoting (Psalm 2 and Psalm 16:10).

Part 3 (38-41). Now Paul's own distinctive understanding of the gospel began to show itself. Unlike Peter, Paul had been a Pharisee. For a Pharisee, the heart of religion was keeping the Law of Moses down to its minutest detail. Every failure added to the weight of one's sin. For every sin forced one to try to make atonement by an even more rigorous keeping of the Law. Thus the Law had become an intolerable burden of life.

So Paul's conclusion was as follows: Jesus was the goal of Jewish history; but He was put to death; yet he conquered death by rising from the grave; and He arose to the end that He might free us from the Law and sin. Therefore, in Christ, it is a whole different story. Christ is the mediator through whom the world is to be saved. Faith in Him, not in the Law, will do more for mankind than the Law ever could; namely, obtain the forgiveness of sins.

If you are on this side of a swollen river and your home is on the other side, and you want to get home, and I tell you I've found a bridge, shouldn't you ask, "Where?"

If I tell you, and you don't use it to get home, don't those on the other side have a right to condemn you?

Paul was telling them that Christ, not the Law, is the bridge. He is the One who forgives sins for all who believe in Him—something the Law could never do.

Perhaps Paul detected some anger at this "slur" of the Mosaic Law, or some cynicism. So Paul warned them not to let what the prophet Habakkuk (609 B.C.) foretold to the Israelites before the Babylonian invasion be fulfilled once again (Hb 1:5).

"Don't be cynical," he said in effect; "you don't have to be a musician to know when someone is on key or off."

Paul's address aroused a general interest. It is always a good sign when people invite you back to speak. Paul and Barnabas were invited back for the following Sabbath.,

Address to the Gentiles (44-52). On the following Sabbath, almost the whole city turned out to hear Paul. Paul's and Barnabas' success filled the Jews with envy; envy caused them to contradict Paul with violent abuse. Paul and Barnabas spoke out boldly and said that since the Jews had rejected the word of God, they would turn to the Gentiles. They did, and the Gentiles were delighted and believed.

There is no fury like envy. The Jews got influential Gentile women, who were Jewish proselytes, to stir up their husbands and the city officials against Paul and Barnabas. Antioch, as a result, became unsafe for them, so they left the city and went to Iconium.

The gospel reveals the hearts of men. Christ is a sign of contradiction. His word, like a two-edged sword, divides. The gospel compels one to take sides, forces a decision. God's word never leaves a person as if finds him. It makes a man better or worse. The good become better; the bad become worse. The superficially bad become good, like the good thief; the superficially good, like the prominent women worshippers who accused the missionaries, become bad. Thus the gospel reveals the hearts of many, (Cp.,Brete Hart's "The Outcasts of Poker Flats.")

Also, we say, "Whatever is received is received according to the disposition of the receiver." The receiver controls input, just as the soil determines the fruitfulness of the seed. Thus the Jews were filled with envy; the Gentiles, with joy and the Holy Spirit.

The incident at Antioch brought Paul and Barnabas to make a momentous decision. Up to this point the mission of the Church had been directed to the Jewish synagogue. Gentiles had been accepted into the Church, but they had come by way of the synagogue. The Ethiopian eunuch, Cornelius, the Greeks at Antioch in Syria—all these had been God-fearing Gentiles who worshipped in the synagogue and studied the Scriptures long before they had heard the gospel. But in Pisidian Antioch, Gentiles came to them who had never been in a synagogue before. They were just as receptive to the gospel as the Jews were hostile. So Paul and Barnabas resolved to turn to these people and to work with them outside the synagogue, if necessary. This was a decisive moment in the development of the Church.

Paul and Barnabas at Iconium (14:1-7). The missionaries followed the great royal highway south and east to Iconium, 80 miles away. Iconium was a big city at the time of Paul, on a plain at the foot of the Taurus Mt. The road connecting Ephesus to the east ran through it.

But the experience of Paul and Barnabas in Antioch was to be repeated again and again for them; first they would preach in the synagogues, be accepted by a few; be rejected by the majority; then they would preach to the Gentiles with many of them accepting Christianity; finally, they would be expelled from the city by Jewish intrigue.

Thus in Iconium Paul and Barnabas entered the Jewish synagogue—some believed, many did not. Those who did not maligned them as evil men. To give lie to the slander, Paul and Barnabas stayed there a long time and spoke out boldly for the Lord. And the Lord confirmed their words by signs and wonders. The result was that the city was divided; some were for the apostles, some were against them. When a plot was hatched against their lives, Paul and Barnabas passed on to Lystra, 25 miles to the southwest.

Paul and Barnabas at Lystra (14:8-20). At Lystra, Paul cured a crippled man, lame from birth. Miracles were like ringing a bell: they summoned crowds to the miracle-workers. The legend of Baucis and Philemon, about Jupiter (Zeus) and Mercury (Hermes) coming in disguise, happened in this area. So the Lycaonians took Paul and Barnabas to be gods come again in disguise. They thought Barnabas, the taller and more dignified of the two, to be Zeus, the father of the gods; and Paul, the more eloquent and the quicker in movement to be Hermes, the messenger of the gods.

Word was sent to the local priest and oxen and garlands were brought to offer sacrifice to Paul and Barnabas. When they realized what was happening, Paul and Barnabas tore their garments and shouted, "What are you doing? We are human just like you. We proclaim the good news to you so that you may turn from idols, dead gods, to the living God, Who made heaven, earth and sea and all that is in them. In the past he let you go your own way. But even then, He gave you a witness of Himself by His goodness in providing the seasons and nourishment that gladdens men's hearts." Even then it was hard to restrain the crown from offering sacrifice to them.

However, it wasn't long before Jews from Antioch and Iconium arrived and stirred up the people against them. Paul was stoned, like Stephen, and left for dead. He survived, but ever afterward bore the scars of that stoning (Gal. 6:17). Apparently his recovery was miraculous. The distance from garlands to stones is short, as was the time from "Hosanna" to "crucify Him." Yet it was from here that Paul was to get his choicest fruit for his ministry, the half-Jew Timothy. Later on, when he returned to Lystra, Timothy became one of his dearest disciples (16:1) The next day Paul and Barnabas left for Derbe, about 40 miles southeast of Lystra.

End of the First Mission (14:21-28). At Derbe they made many converts. Apparently the mission there was very successful and uneventful. At Derbe, Paul and Barnabas were on the southeastern border of the Roman province of Galatia. A good road lay ahead of them to Tarsus and Syrian Antioch their home base. Yet instead of taking that shortcut home, Paul and Barnabas were so concerned about the little groups of believers from whom they had to flee that they backtracked and in the face of great danger revisited the churches they had founded in Lystra, Iconium, Antioch. Either because new magistrates were in office or because they worked in secret they escaped persecution.

Paul's evangelization was not haphazard. He strengthened the disciples and exhorted them to stand firm in the faith by reminding them that "it is necessary to undergo many hardships to enter the kingdom of God." Then he set up structures, appointing presbyters, leaders, who would help them survive persecution. He wanted them to be self-governing, self-sustaining, self-propagating.

Then they traveled through Pisidia and reached Pamphylia. At Perga they preached, probably Paul's health permitted him to do this now. From there they went to Attalia, the seaport of Perga; took a boat and returned to Syrian Antioch in the year 49 A.D., four years after their departure on this, Paul's first great missionary journey. At Antioch, they made a full report to the whole church there.

The wording of their report was interesting. They did not speak of what they had done. Rather, they spoke of "what God had done with them." They didn't say, "Oh, did we suffer! Boy, was it rough and tough." Rather they related how God had opened the door of faith to the Gentiles—the door closed by the Jews. But a door opened to the Gentiles and never closed since.

Jesus said, "I am the door." Faith is the key that unlocks the door. Faith is necessary for salvation just as a rope and bucket are to draw water from a well. Faith turns rocky soil into fertile soil, makes one receptive to God.

After their report, Paul and Barnabas went right back to work in Antioch. Apostles never rest.

Acts 15:1-35

15 Council of Jerusalem [1] Some who had come down from Judea were instructing the brothers, "Unless you are circumcised according to the Mosaic practice, you cannot be saved." [2] Because there arose no little dissension and debate by Paul and Barnabas with them, it was decided that Paul, Barnabas, and some of the others should go up to Jerusalem to the apostles and presbyters about this question. [3] They were sent on their journey by the church, and passed through Phoenicia and Samaria telling of the conversion of the Gentiles, and brought great joy to all the brothers. [4] When they arrived in Jerusalem, they were welcomed by the church, as well as by the apostles and the presbyters, and they reported what God had done with them. [5] But some from the party of the Pharisees who had become believers stood up and said, "It is necessary to circumcise them and direct them to observe the Mosaic law."

[6] The apostles and the presbyters met together to see about this matter. [7] After much debate had taken place, Peter got up and said to them, "My brothers, you are well aware that from early days God made his choice among you that through my mouth the Gentiles would hear the word of the gospel and believe. [8] And God, who knows the heart, bore witness by granting them the Holy Spirit just as he did us. [9] He made no distinction between us and them, for by faith he purified their hearts. [10] Why, then, are you now putting God to the test by placing on the shoulders of the disciples a yoke that neither our ancestors nor we have been able to bear? [11] On the contrary, we believe that we are saved through the grace of the Lord Jesus, in the same way as they." [12] The whole assembly fell silent, and they listened while Paul and Barnabas described the signs and wonders God had worked among the Gentiles through them.

James on Dietary Law. [13] After they had fallen silent, James responded. "My brothers, listen to me. [14] Symeon has described how God first concerned himself with acquiring from among the Gentiles a people for his name. [15] The words of the prophets agree with this, as is written:

[16] 'After this I shall return
and rebuild the fallen hut of David;
from its ruins I shall rebuild it
and raise it up again,
[17] so that the rest of humanity may seek out the Lord,
even all the Gentiles on whom my name is invoked.
Thus says the Lord who accomplishes these things,
[18] known from of old.'

[19] It is my judgment, therefore, that we ought to stop troubling the Gentiles who turn to God, [20] but tell them by letter to avoid pollution from idols, unlawful marriage, the meat of strangled animals, and blood. [21] For Moses, for generations now, has had those who proclaim him in every town, as he has been read in the synagogues every sabbath."

Letter of the Apostles [22] Then the apostles and presbyters, in agreement with the whole church, decided to choose representation and to send them to Antioch with Paul and Barnabas. The ones chosen were Judas, who was called Barsabbas, and Silas, leaders among the brothers. [23] This is the letter delivered by them: "The apostles and the presbyters, your brothers, to the brothers in Antioch, Syria, and Cilicia of Gentile origin: greetings. [24] Since we have heard that some of our number [who went out] without any mandate from us have upset you with their teachings and disturbed your peace of mind, [25] we have with one accord decided to choose representatives and to send them to you along with our beloved Barnabas and Paul, [26] who have dedicated their lives to the name of our Lord Jesus Christ. [27] So we are sending Judas and Silas who will also convey this same message by word of mouth: [28] 'It is the decision of the Holy Spirit and of us not to place on you any burden beyond these necessities, [29] namely, to abstain from meat sacrificed to idols, from blood, from meats of strangled animals, and from unlawful marriage. If you keep free of these, you will be doing what is right. Farewell.'"

Delegates at Antioch [30] And so they were sent on their journey. Upon their arrival in Antioch they called the assembly together and delivered the letter. [31] When the people read it, they were delighted with the exhortation. [32] Judas and Silas, who were themselves prophets, exhorted and strengthened the brothers with many words. [33] After they had spent some time there, they were sent off with greetings of peace from the brothers to those who had commissioned them [34] [35] But Paul and Barnabas remained in Antioch teaching and proclaiming with many others the word of the Lord.

Facts on Acts

CHAPTER 11

Council of Jerusalem—50 A.D.

(Acts 15)

Not all shared in the joy that the door of faith had been opened to the Gentiles. Paul's missionary activity caused a problem. Missions do create problems, like the need for men, money, prayer, adjustments, and so on. Only dead churches have no problems.

On his mission, Paul had insisted that faith alone in Christ saves; there was no need for observing the Mosaic law. Soon some converted Pharisees from Jerusalem came down to Antioch and took exception to Paul's methods. They taught that unless Gentiles were circumcised according to the Mosaic law they could not be saved.

This started a veritable donnybrook. Paul and Barnabas protested vigorously. But recognizing the authority of the Church in Jerusalem, it was decided that they and some of the others (Titus was probably one of these—Gal. 2:3) should go up to Jerusalem to the apostles and presbyters about this question. On the way, they told everyone about the conversion of the Gentiles and all rejoiced. At Jerusalem they were welcomed by the Church, as well as by the apostles and presbyters, and they reported what God had done with them (Galatians 2:1-9). Again the same old converted Pharisees objected. So the apostles and presbyters called a Council.[1]

Battles often begin with skirmishes by light troops that decide really nothing, except to clear the ground for the onset of the battalions. These decide the outcome of the battle. So here after long debating, after the matter had been thoroughly aired and nothing was decided, then the leaders spoke: Peter, Paul and Barnabas and James.

Peter arose and for the third time told the story of the conversion of Cornelius. As the ship of the Church sails toward the Gentiles, Peter is at the helm. As always, Peter spoke with effect: he reaffirmed the principle: "we are all saved through the grace of the Lord Jesus." The whole assembly quieted down.

The assembly, now disposed by Peter, was ready to hear Paul and Barnabas. They simply narrated what God had done for the Gentiles. Both were confirmed Jews: Paul, a Pharisee; and Barnabas, a Levite. So they would never have surrendered any just claim of Judaism had not God Himself intervened. The fact was the gist of their argument.

Finally, James spoke. He was the Bishop of Jerusalem and "brother of the Lord." As such, he probably had chaired the meeting. He was a staunch defender of the Hebrew Christian. He was so conscientious an observer of the Mosaic law, that not even the most exacting rabbi could find fault with his orthodoxy. His decision, therefore, had great weight.

James on Dietary Law (15:13-21). Peter, Paul and Barnabas had told what God had done for the Gentiles; James told what God had said in the Scriptures on this matter. He backed up Symeon's (note James used the Hebrew name) story about Cornelius by quoting Amos 9:11-12. Then he recommended that the Gentiles be left alone and a letter be sent freeing them from circumcision and the

---

1 Tradition tells us that Mary died in Jerusalem in 49 A.D. (on the eve of the Council) at the age of 69, and that all the apostles were recalled from their far-flung missions to be present for her last hours on earth.

In Acts the word "apostles" is repeatedly mentioned in the ensuing Council of Jerusalem to suggest that many of the apostles were there. Their presence would help explain the decision of the Council, for in their missions they had met many Gentiles; and, like Peter regarding Cornelius, they had received them without imposing the Law of Moses.

Mosaic law. There were only two exceptions: the Gentiles were to observe only those dietary regulations that would prevent Jew and Gentile from eating together, so that they could celebrate the Eucharist together; and to abstain from sexual immorality (probably illegal marriages). In other words, James recommended that the Gentiles observe only those rules and regulations needed to safeguard the community and its basic unit, the family.

Letter of the Apostles (15:22-29). It is significant that the first Council of the Church was one that freed from laws, not one that imposed them. It solved the great problem of the early Church by declaring that it was not necessary to become a Jew in order to become a Christian. Working out the consequences of this principle would take a long time. Throughout his missionary life, Paul was plagued by Judaizers, who kept insisting that Gentile converts be compelled to keep the Mosaic law; they were a thorn in his side, especially in regard to the Galatians.

The Council decided to send Judas, called Barsabbas, and Silas to bring the letter to the Church at Antioch. Those two would vouch for its authenticity. The letter began with the usual greeting and the introduction of the letter bearers, Judas and Silas. Then it set forth the Council's decision. It prefaced this with the words, "It is the decision of the Holy Spirit and of us.." The Spirit guides the Church and the Church echoes the Spirit.

Controversy is unavoidable in the life of the Church. Controversy is the sign of life, activity, growth. It is preferable to the peace of the graveyard.

One of the best ways to settle controversy is by full discussion and personal conferences, like a council. In numbers there is safety.

St. Iraeneus enunciated a basic principle to observe in controversies. He said: *In certis — unitas; in incertis — libertas: sed in imnibus — caritas.* Which means: in issues that are certain, let there be unity; in issues that are uncertain, or controversial, let there be liberty; but in all issues, let there be charity.

Acts 15:36 - 16:40

V. The Mission of Paul to The Ends of The Earth

Paul and Barnabas Separate [36] After some time, Paul said to Barnabas, "Come, let us make a return visit to see how the brothers are getting on in all the cities where we proclaimed the word of the Lord." [37] Barnabas wanted to take with them also John, who was called Mark, [38] but Paul insisted that they should not take with them someone who had deserted them at Pamphylia and who had not continued with them in their work. [39] So sharp was their disagreement that they separated. Barnabas took Mark and sailed to Cyprus. [40] But Paul chose Silas and departed after being commended by the brothers to the grace of the Lord. He traveled through Syria and Cilicia bringing strength to the churches.

16 Paul in Lycaonia: Timothy [1] He reached [also] Derbe and *Lystra where there was a disciple named Timothy,* the son of a Jewish woman who was a believer, but his father was a Greek. [2] The brothers in Lystra and Iconium spoke highly of him, [3] and Paul wanted him to come along with him. On account of the Jews of that region, Paul had him circumcised, for they all knew that his father was a Greek. [4] As they traveled from city to city, they handed on to the people for observance *the decisions reached by the apostles and presbyters in Jerusalem.* [5] Day after day the churches grew stronger in faith and increased in number.

Through Asia Minor [6] They traveled through the Phrygian and Galatian territory *because they had been prevented by the Holy Spirit from preaching the message in the province of Asia.* [7] When they came to Mysia, they tried to go in into *Bithynia* but the Spirit of Jesus did not allow them, [8] so they crossed through Mysia and came down to *Troas.* [9] During [the] night Paul had a vision. A Macedonian stood before him and implored him with these words, "Come over to Macedonia and help us." [10] When he had seen the vision, *we* sought passage to Macedonia at once, concluding that God had called us to proclaim the good news to them.

Into Europe [11] We set sail from Troas, making a straight run for Samothrace, and on the next day to Neapolis, [12] and from there to *Philippi*, a leading city in that district of Macedonia and a Roman colony. We spent some time in that city. [13] On the sabbath we went outside the city gate along the river where we thought there would be a place of prayer. We sat and spoke with the women who had gathered there. [14] One of them, a woman named *Lydia*, a dealer in purple cloth, from the city of Thyatira, a worshiper of God listened, and the Lord opened her heart to pay attention to what Paul was saying. [15] After she and her household had been baptized, she offered us an invitation, "If you consider me a believer in the Lord, come and stay at my home." and she prevailed on us.

Imprisonment at Philippi [16] As we were going to the place of prayer, we met a *slave girl* with an oracular spirit, who used to bring a large profit to her owners through her fortune-telling. [17] She began to follow Paul and us, shouting, "These people are slaves of the Most High God, who proclaim to you a way of salvation." [18] She did this for many days. Paul became annoyed, turned and said to the spirit, "I command you in the name of Jesus Christ to come out of her." Then it came out at that moment.

[19] When her owners saw that their hope of profit was gone, they seized Paul and Silas and dragged them to the public square before the local authorities. [20] They brought them before the magistrates and said, "These people are *Jews* and are disturbing our city [21] and are advocating customs that are not lawful for us Romans to adopt or practice." [22] The crowd joined in the attack on them, and the magistrates had them stripped and ordered them to be beaten with rods. [23] After inflicting many blows on them, they threw them into prison and instructed the jailer to guard them securely. [24] When he received these instructions, he put them in the innermost cell and secured their feet to a stake.

Deliverance from Prison [25] About midnight, while Paul and Silas were praying and singing hymns to God as the prisoners listened. [26] there was suddenly such a severe earthquake that the foundations of the jail shook; all the doors flew open, and the chains of all were pulled loose. [27] When the jailer woke up and saw the prison doors wide open, he drew [his] sword and was about the kill himself, thinking that the prisoners had escaped. [28] But Paul shouted out in a loud voice. "Do no harm to yourself; we are all here." [29] He asked for a light and rushed in and, trembling with fear, he fell down before Paul and Silas. [30] Then he brought them out and said, "Sirs, what must I do to be saved?" [31] And they said, "Believe in the Lord Jesus and you and your household will be saved." [32] So they spoke the word of the Lord to him and to everyone in his house. [33] He took them in at that hour of the night and bathed their wounds; then he and all his family were baptized at once. [34] He brought them up into his house and provided a meal and with his household rejoiced at having come to faith in God.

[35] But when it was day, the magistrates sent the lictors with the order, "Release those men." [36] The jailer reported the[se] words to Paul, "The magistrates have sent orders that you be released. Now, then, come out and go in peace." [37] But Paul said to them, "They have beaten us publicly, even though we are Roman citizens and have not been tried, and have thrown us into prison. And now, are they going to release us secretly? By no means. Let them come themselves and lead us out." [38] The lictors reported these words to the magistrates, and they became alarmed when they heard that they were Roman citizens. [39] So they came and placated them, and let them out and asked that they leave the city. [40] When they had come out of the prison, they went to Lydia's house where they saw and encouraged the brothers; and then they left.

Acts 17:1-34

17 Paul in Thessalonica [1] When they took the road through *Amphipolis* and *Apollonia*, they reached *Thessalonica*, where there was a synagogue of the Jews. [2] Following his usual custom, Paul joined them, and for three sabbaths he entered into discussion with them from the scriptures. [3] expounding and demonstrating that the Messiah had to suffer and rise from the dead, and that "This is the Messiah, Jesus, whom I proclaim to you." [4] Some of them were convinced and joined Paul and Silas; so, too, a great number of Greeks who were worshippers, and not a few of the prominent women. [5] *But the Jews became jealous* and recruited some worthless men loitering in the public square, formed a mob, and set the city in turmoil. They marched on the house of Jason, intending to bring them before the people's assembly. [6] When they could not find them, they dragged Jason and some of the brothers before the city magistrates, shouting, "These people who have been creating a disturbance all over the world have now come here, [7] and Jason welcomed them. They all act in opposition to the decrees of Caesar and *claim instead that there is another king, Jesus.*" [8] They stirred up the crowd and the city magistrates who, upon hearing these charges, [9] took a surety payment from Jason and the others before releasing them.

Paul in Beroca [10] The brothers immediately sent Paul and Silas to Beroca during the night. Upon arrival they went to the synagogue of the Jews. [11] These Jews *were more fairminded than those in Thessalonica*, for they received the word with all willingness and *examined the scriptures daily* to determine whether these things were so. [12] Many of them became believers, as did not a few of the influential Greek women and men. [13] But when the Jews of Thessalonica learned that the word of God had now been proclaimed by Paul in Beroea also; they came there too to cause a commotion and stir up the crowds. [14] So the brothers at once sent Paul on his way to the seacoast, while *Silas* and *Timothy* remained behind. [15] After Paul's escorts had taken him to Athens, they came away with instructions for Silas and Timothy to join him as soon as possible.

Paul in Athens [16] While Paul was waiting for them in Athens, he grew exasperated at the sight of the city full of idols. [17] So he debated in the synagogue with the Jews and with the worshipers, and daily in the public square with whoever happened to be there. [18] Even some of the Epicurean and Stoic philosophers engaged him in discussion. Some asked, "What is this scavenger trying to do?" Others said, "He sounds like a promoter of foreign deities." because he was preaching about 'Jesus' and 'Resurrection.' [19] They took him and led him to the Areopagus and said, "May we learn what this new teaching is that you speak of? [20] For you bring some strange notions to our ears; we should like to know what these things mean,." [21] Now all the Athenians as well as the foreigners residing there used their time for nothing else but telling or hearing something new.

Paul's Speech at the Areopagus [22] Then Paul stood up at the Areopagus and said: "You Athenians, I see that in every respect you are very religious. [23] For as I walked around looking carefully at your shrines, I even discovered an altar inscribed, 'To an Unknown God.' That therefore you unknowingly worship, I proclaim to you. [24] The God who made the world and all that is in it, the Lord of heaven and earth, does not dwell in sanctuaries made by human hands. [25] nor is he served by human hands because he needs anything. Rather it is he who gives to everyone life and breath and everything. [26] *He made from one the whole human race to dwell* on the entire surface of the earth, and he fixed the ordered seasons and the boundaries of their regions. [27] so that people might seek God, even perhaps grope for him and find him, though indeed he is not far from any one of us. [28] For 'In Him we live and move and have our being' as even some of your poets have said, 'For we too are his offspring.' [29] Since therefore we are the offspring of God, we ought not to think that the divinity is like an image fashioned from gold, silver, or stone by human art and imagination. [30] God has overlooked the times of ignorance, but now he demands that all people everywhere repent [31] because he has established a day on which he will 'judge the world with justice' through a man he has appointed, and he has provided confirmation for all by raising him from the dead."

[32] When they heard about *resurrection of the dead*, some began to scoff, but others said, "we should like to hear you

on this some other time." [33] And so Paul left them. [34] But some did join him, and became believers. Among them were Dionysius, a member of the Court of Areopagus, a woman named Damaris, and others with them.

Acts 18:1-23

Paul in Corinth [1] After he left Athens and went to Corinth. [2] There he met a Jew named Aquila, a native of Pontus, who had recently come from Italy with his wife Priscilla because Claudius had ordered all the Jews to leave Rome. He went to visit them [3] and, because he practiced the same trade, stayed with them and worked, for they were tentmakers by trade. [4] Every Sabbath, he entered into discussions in the synagogue, attempting to convince both Jews and Greeks.

[5] When Silas and Timothy came down from Macedonia, Paul began to occupy himself totally with preaching the word, testifying to the Jews that the Messiah was Jesus. [6] When they opposed him and reviled him, he shook out his garments and said to them, "Your blood be on your heads! I am clear of responsibility. From now on I will go to the Gentiles." [7] So he left there and went to a house belonging to a man named *Titus Justus*, a worshiper of God; his house was next to a synagogue. [8] *Crispus*, the synagogue official, came to believe in the Lord along with his entire household, and many of the Corinthians who heard believed and were baptized. [9] One night in a vision the Lord said to Paul, "Do not be afraid. Go on speaking, and do not be silent, [10] for I am with you. No one will attack and harm you, for I have many people in this city." [11] He settled there for a year and a half and taught the word of God among them.

Accusations before Gallio [12] But when Gallio was proconsul of Achaia, the Jews rose up together against Paul and brought him to the tribunal, [13] saying, "This man is inducing people to worship God contrary to the law." [14] When Paul was about to reply, Gallio spoke to the Jews, "If it were a matter of some crime or malicious fraud, I should with reason hear the complaint of you Jews; [15] but since it is a question of arguments over doctrine and titles and your own law, see to it yourselves. I do not wish to be a judge of such matters." [16] And he drove them away from the tribunal. [17] They all seized *Sosthenes*, the synagogue official, and beat him in full view of the tribunal. But none of this was of concern to Gallio.

Return to Syrian Antioch [18] Paul remained for quite some time, and after saying farewell to the brothers he sailed for Syria, together with Priscilla and Aquila. At *Cenchreae* he had his hair cut because he had taken a vow. [19] When they reached Ephesus, he left them there, while he entered the synagogue and held discussions with the Jews. [20] Although they asked him to stay for a longer time, he did not consent, [21] but as he said farewell he promised, "*I shall come back* to you again, God willing." Then he set sail from Ephesus. [22] Upon landing at Caesarea, he went up and greeted the church and then went down to Antioch. [23] After staying there for some time, he left and traveled in orderly sequence through the Galatian country and Phrygia, bringing strength to all the disciples.

Facts on Acts

CHAPTER 12

Paul's Second Missionary Journey 50 - 53 A.D.

2,500 miles

(Acts 15:36-18:23)

Following the Council of Jerusalem, Paul returned to Antioch for a few months. Peter followed soon after. It was probably on this occasion that Paul confronted Peter and upbraided him for giving in to human respect by ceasing to eat with Gentiles (Gal. 2:11-14). Peter, as always, humbly accepted the rebuke.

Soon after, Peter went into northern Asia Minor—Bithynia, Pontus, and Cappadocia—and evangelized these provinces till the end of the reign of Claudius (54 A.D.). After Claudius' death, Peter returned to Rome.

After Peter had left Antioch, Paul also started out on his second missionary journey. It began with a fright, a very bitter and sharp disagreement (*paroxysmos*), between Paul and Barnabas over John Mark. Barnabas wanted to bring Mark along, Paul refused—he would have nothing to do with the deserter in Pamphylia. So they split up: Barnabas took Mark with himself to Cyprus: and Silas took Barnabas' place; then at Lystra, Paul picked up Timothy to take Mark's place.

One of the great problems in all Church work is getting along with others. Sometimes it is all right to agree to disagree. Under the kind tutelage of Barnabas, Mark regained his self-respect and became a great evangelist and was later reconciled with Paul. When hearts are good, even quarrels work together unto good.

The Council of Jerusalem had settled the major issues raised by Paul's first missionary journey. The big question had been: "Could Gentiles be saved apart from the observances of the Mosaic law?" The Council had given a resounding "Yes, they can." The doors now were wide open for the unlimited growth of the Church.

Luke is now ready to make Paul the central figure of the second half of Acts. Peter has made his exit.[1] Barnabas disappears to Cyprus. The apostles at Jerusalem are mentioned for a last time. Luke chose Paul as the one best suited to illustrate the spread of the good news and the fulfillment of Christ's command to go teach all nations. As we shall see, it will not be Paul, but the Holy Spirit who will determine the course of his second journey.

In golf, "follow through" is most important. So it is with missionary work. The architect must see not only to the foundations, but also to the superstructure. Paul was concerned about the churches he had founded on his first missionary journey. Leaving Antioch, accompanied by Silas, he traveled through Syria and Cilicia strengthening the churches there.

Paul in Lycaonia: Timothy (16:1-5). Next he revisited the Lycaonian cities of Derbe, then Lystra. At Lystra Paul found his dearest disciple, Timothy, whose mother, Eunice was Jewish and whose father was Greek. Everyone spoke so highly of Timothy that Paul invited him to join him and Silas on this missionary tour, in order to take Mark's place. Because of the Jews of the area and to facilitate Timothy's ministry to Jews, Paul circumcised him. (Paul had no objection to circumcising a Jew). Then the trio traveled on

---

1. At the death of Claudius in 54, the edict banishing Jews from Rome presumably lapsed. Very likely Peter returned to Rome at this time and stayed there for three years to 57 A.D. Mark joined Peter at this time and wrote his gospel.

    Peter left Rome in 57 to 62 to go to Bithynia, Pontus and Cappadocia to strengthen the churches there. Mark went to Alexandria and founded the church there, 58-62.

    In 62 Peter returned to Rome and recalled Mark from Alexandria. In 67 Peter was martyred. Mark returned to Alexandria and he himself was martyred there in 68 A.D. (See appendix 1)

from city to city, Paul told everyone about the decisions of the Council of Jerusalem, expanding and strengthening the churches.

Through Asia Minor (16:22-29). After Paul had finished revisiting the churches of his first mission, he was at a loss as to where else to go. He headed for Ephesus, but the Holy Spirit stopped him. So he traveled north through Phrygian and Galatian territory. It was probably on this occasion that Paul evangelized the Galatians.

When he came to Mysia about 150 miles from the seacoast, Paul stood with Bithynia on his right—wealthy, populous, favorite resort of emperors; and Asia Minor on his left with its great ports and cities, like Ephesus, Sardis, Phildadelphia, Smyrna, and vast populations sunk in idolatry. Both fields seemed ripe for the harvest, yet the Holy Spirit prohibited him from going to these spots at this particular time.,

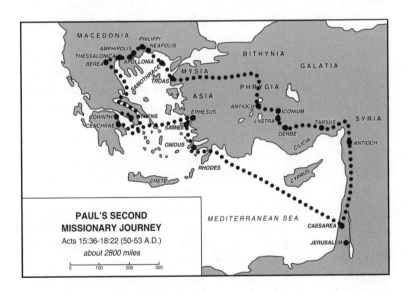

PAUL'S SECOND MISSIONARY JOURNEY
Acts 15:36-18:22 (50-53 A.D.)
about 2800 miles

"So they crossed through Mysia and came down to Troas" (13 miles from the site of ancient Troy), where Luke joined them. Troas was a great mercantile city. What was Paul to do now; he couldn't go east and to the west was the sea?

Well, that very night Paul had a vision. A Macedonian stood before him and implored, "Come over to Macedonia and help us."

Alexander the Great was a Macedonian. He had conquered the world and dreamed of making the East and the West one world. Philippi was named after his father, Thessalonica was named after his half-sister. Troas was named after him, for its full name was Alexandrian Troas. Could it have been Alexander who begged Paul to come to Macedonia, to make the world one? It might well have been. No matter. A Macedonian came to Paul; and Paul reasoned that God wanted the faith brought to Europe.

Thus Luke wrote: "When he had seen the vision, we sought passage to Macedonia at once." This is the first of the so called "we" sections in Acts, where Luke writes as one of Paul's companions. Some think a bodily ailment kept Paul from going to Ephesus or to Bithynia and caused him to sojourn in Galatia and found churches there (Gal. 4:12-16). Paul saw this as the Spirit of God and somehow got word to Luke, a doctor, to meet him at Troas.

Why did the Holy Spirit bypass Asia Minor and Bithynia? It perhaps was not yet ready for the harvest. A farmer tells his workers to reap here but not there, because such a field is not ripe yet. Later Paul went to Ephesus; and Peter wrote to the churches in Pontus, Bithynia, etc. No doubt success in the West would make it easier for Paul to succeed in the East. So at this time the Spirit sent him West, to Europe.

Into Europe (16:11-15). It was probably early in the year 51 A.D. that the missionaries set sail from Troas, went to Samothrace, then landed at Neapolis. From there, Paul, following his custom of evangelizing in the large cities, went directly to Philippi, which was a leading city in Macedonia and a Roman colony. Philip, the father of Alexander the Great, in 358 B.C., enlarged the old town of Krenides, place of small springs, and fortified it against the Thracians and renamed it after himself—Philippi.

It was at Philippi that one of the great decisive battles of history was fought in 42 B.C., when Octavius Caesar and Marc Antony defeated the assassins of Julius Caesar, Brutus and Cassius. Later, Octavius made the city a Roman colony.

When Paul came to Philippi, he found no crowds waiting. He had to fend for himself. How sparing God is in His directions! It is so that one might have room to cooperate. Don't we spoil children by doing too much for them?

Apparently, there was no Jewish synagogue in Philippi, so on the Sabbath Paul and his companions went outside the city to a place of prayer by a river, possibly the Gangites, a mile and quarter from the city. They sat down and spoke with the women there—no preaching, just talking. And the first convert in the West was a woman, Lydia. Christianity never degrades women. She is always open to them. For a woman was the mother of Jesus. Many of His followers were women. He Himself appeared first to women on Easter. And here again, in the mission field, the good news in Europe was brought first to women.

Lydia was probably a God-fearing Gentile; perhaps a widow, for no mention is made of her husband. Being from Thyatira in Asia Minor, a great dyeing center since the days of Homer, she was a dealer in purple cloth, and so a wealthy woman. Purple dye was costly; once more costly than gold. Only kings wore linen dyed purple. In the days of decadent Rome, the nobles and very wealthy also began to wear it, as did Dives in the parable of our Lord. The dye was discovered by accident. A dog had been eating a Conchilis or Purpura, a shell-fish. Its mouth as a result was stained all purple and that was how this costly dye came to be discovered.

Lydia, undoubtedly, worshipped the true God, for she did not do business on the Sabbath, and she was here at the riverside for prayer. God rewarded her goodness by giving her true faith. She listened to Paul, and God opened her heart to what he was saying. As always, man works from without, God works from within. If God does not work from within, in vain would man work from without. That is why evangelists must be persons of prayer.

Lydia and her whole household was baptized. To baptize entire households was a common practice in Acts. This is significant, because in households there had to be infants and children. The implication is that infant baptism was practiced in the early Church. Lydia insisted that Paul and his companions stay at her home. They did.

Imprisonment at Philippi (16:16-24). Lydia belonged to the upper class; but the next person Paul ran into was a slave girl, belonging to the lowest class.

The slave girl was clairvoyant, maybe a ventriloquist, so she was thought to have a Python spirit. The Python was the serpent that guarded the Delphic oracle. Then it came to designate "a spirit" that pronounced oracles." The girl, by wild and shrill cries, imitated the priestesses of Delphi; and so people attributed her clairvoyance to a Python spirit. Evil men used her to make money through her fortune-telling.

For many days, the slave girl followed Paul and his companions and shouted out after them, "These people are slaves of the Most High God, who proclaim to you a way of salvation." Finally, Paul annoyed, ordered the spirit to leave her. And it did!

Even though her testimony was true, Paul would have none of it, for he knew an evil spirit could be up to no good. Then, too, he was annoyed to see the degradation of a human being by the demon and her exploitation by evil men whose sole concern was gain regardless of the harm to the girl or to people.

When her owners saw that their hope of profit was gone, they attacked Paul and Silas and denounced them to the Roman authorities. So long as the gospel does not interfere with bad men's money-making, it will be tolerated. But let it hit pocketbooks, and all hell will break loose. These greedy, evil men, liars and racists, accused Paul and Silas of being Jews and of disturbing the peace. As a result, the apostles were punished with more than usual severity, scourged with rods and put in a dungeon, in stock — "insolently treated" (1Thess. 2:2)

Deliverance from Prison (16:25-39). Lydia was from the highest class; the slave girl, from the lowest class; now, Luke presents a man from the middle class—a jailer.

About midnight, Paul and Silas could not sleep from the pain of their scourging, so they prayed, for they needed comfort; and they sang hymns, for comfort was given. In answer to their prayer and song, a severe earthquake occurred, shaking the foundations of the jail, opening all the doors, and pulling loose the chains binding the prisoners. How wonderfully God answers prayer; how vehemently He hates seeing persons bound in chains.

When the jailer discovered the gates were opened, he was going to kill himself. (Herod executed the guards when Peter escaped.) Paul shouted, "Do no harm to yourself." The jailer called for a light, rushed into the cell, and fell trembling at the feet of Paul and Silas, and believed. The conduct of the apostles, the earthquake, Paul's exhortation, had opened up his heart, and he said, "Sirs, what must I do to be saved?" Saved from what? A greater danger than death.

Paul answered, "Believe in the Lord Jesus and you and your household will be saved." Since he had not heard of the Lord Jesus, Paul proceeded to announce the word of God. If a man has a room on the third story of a hotel and there is no fire escape, only a rope ladder, he believes that if there is a fire the rope ladder will help him escape. So the jailer believed in the Lord Jesus. He bathed their wounds; then he and his whole family were baptized (again there must have been some infant baptisms). After that, he led them into his house, spread a table before them, fed them and celebrated his new-found faith in God.

The next day the magistrates sent men to release Paul and his companions. Paul refused to leave the city to teach civil authorities that in persecuting men for their faith, they offend the laws of God and of men. He insisted on leaving the city with dignity for the sake of the gospel. When freed, he took his time. He went to the house of Lydia, encouraged the brothers there, then left Philippi, under the safe guidance of Luke and Timothy.

And that was how the faith came to Europe. It took in a cross-section of society: an upper class woman, a lower class girl, and a middle class jailer. From that mustard seed grew European civilization. Take out of the great cities of Europe everything Catholic and you will have only a shell. Remove the great cathedrals: Notre Dame of Paris, Cologne of Germany, St. Peter's of Rome; take Christian art out of the art galleries of Europe; in music leave out Mozart, Handel, Bach, Beethoven, Haydn, Brahms—and what do you have left. All from a tiny seed planted by Paul. Only God knows how far little actions done for God will go.

Paul in Thessalonica (17:1-9). After Paul and Silas left Philippi, they traveled 30 miles to Amphipolis (a city encircled by a great bend of a river, hence its name). Since the city had no synagogue, no means of addressing Jew or Gentile, Paul left the very next day for Appolonia, 30 miles away. The great tragedian Euripides was buried in this area. From there, Paul went south 37 miles to Thessalonica, capital of Macedonia. The city was named after Alexander the Great's half sister. She happened to be born on the day Philip had won a great victory (nike) in Thessaly, so he named her Thessalonica. Here Cicero spent his exile. Here the Emperor Theodosius massacred 7,000 people, for which St., Ambrose kept him out of the cathedral of Milan for eight months.

At Thessalonica there was a synagogue of the Jews. For three sabbaths, Paul expounded the Scriptures there. Between Sabbaths, Paul worked so as not to be a burden to any one (1Thess 2:9). He wished to distinguish himself from other traveling preachers, who used their office for personal gain.

In the synagogue, he demonstrated that the Messiah had to suffer, die, and rise from the dead. Then he argued that this Jesus whom he proclaimed suffered and died and rose from the dead and so is the Messiah. Many God-fearing Greeks and prominent women believed; but this only stirred up the envy of the Jews.

Envy is a base passion; so it never hesitates to use base means—for instance, Cain against Abel, Saul against David, Haman against Mordecai, the devil against mankind. Here the Jews used the riff-raff of the city, together with a pack of lies, to incite the people against Paul. They could not get their hands on Paul and Silas, so they attacked Jason their host. They were too late, for the faith had already taken root in Thessalonica. The case was settled by having Jason pay a find.

Paul in Beroea (17:10-15). During the night, the brothers sent Paul and Silas to Beroea, 60 miles southwest of Thessalonica. Persecution in one city led to the preaching of the gospel in the next city. In Beroea there was a synagogue. The Jews here were more noble than those in Thessalonica. The test of nobleness is good listening. The Beroeans welcomed the message of Paul with enthusiasm. They studied the Scriptures with him to verify his preaching. One obstacle was the crucifixion of the Messiah. So Paul must have had them study Isaiah 53. Many believed; among them, influential Greek women and men.

But Jewish hostility was so deep that the Thessalonian Jews pursued Paul to Beroea. Paul was the focus of their venom. They felt he was a heretic, who had to be stopped at all costs. A lesser man would have given up. Not Paul. He assigned Silas to the Church in Beroea and then left by sea for Athens, virtually a hunted fugitive.

Paul in Athens (17:16-21). Paul was alone in Athens, a city dedicated to the virgin goddess of wisdom, Athena. In her honor the Parthenon (the Greek word for "virgin") was built atop the Acropolis of Phidias and Pericles, when Greece was in her glory (444-436 B.D.)

While waiting for Silas, Luke and Timothy to join him, the restless Paul was exasperated by the rampant polytheism. Athens for 550 years had been not only the intellectual center of the ancient world, but also its religious center. In Athens there were more statues than in all the rest of Greece together. So Paul debated with the Jews in their synagogues, and in the public square with anybody else who would listen.

In Athens, there were two schools of philosophy; the Epicureans, followers of Epicurus (342-271 B.C.), who were materialists and hedonists; and the Stoics, followers of Zeno (335-263 B.C.), who were pantheists and fatalists.

They engaged Paul in debate. Some called him "a scavenger" - literally, a seed-picker, a chattering sparrow, a man talking nonsense that he had picked up somewhere, as birds do seeds. They misunderstood Paul's reference to the resurrection to mean a goddess named Anastasis, that is, Resurrection. And so they accused him of promoting foreign deities: Jesus and Resurrection.

However, the Athenians had "itching ears" — "they used their time for nothing else but telling or hearing something new." So Paul was led to the Areopagus (the hill of the god Ares or Mars), where Themistocles had rallied the West against the Persians. The Hill was just below the Acropolis and to the west of it. There Paul preached. At Philippi the jailer had asked, "What must I do to be saved?" The Athenians were only curious, "we should like to know what these things mean."

Paul's Speech at the Areopagus (17:22-34). Here Paul tempered his speech to his audience. Athens was a university city—a city of intellectuals. So Paul used a philosophical approach and quoted their own authorities, not Scripture.

To gain their goodwill, Paul commended them, "I see that in every respect you are very religious." The essential error of all false religions is a false view of God.

So Paul explained that God was not one made, but the Maker of heaven and earth and all that is in them. From one stock He made the entire human race. Because He made us, they seek Him. But like blind men, they grope in the darkness of ignorance, even though He is not far from anyone for "In Him we live and move and have our being." as Epimenides of Knossos (6th century B.C.) wrote.

Secondly, Paul went on, because God made us, we are His offspring, as the poet Aratus of Cilicia (3rd century B.C.) had said. "Can the Maker be less than the thing he made? If we are flesh and blood, how can we reduce God to golden, lifeless images?"

Thirdly, Paul warned that the time for ignorance was past. God forgave the past follies of mankind because of ignorance, but now He demands that all people everywhere repent. For life is not ended at death, as the Epicureans say; nor is death our absorbtion into God, as the Stoics say. Rather, life is a journey to judgment. And the judge is a man whom God raised from the dead—your unknown God, Jesus.

In other words, Paul depicted the correct view of God: in relation to the world; its Maker; in relation to man: His offspring; in relations to sin: an offense against a personal God, therefore, repent; in relation to salvation: accept Christ, who proved by the resurrection He is God.

In general, Paul's talk was a failure. Some scoffed. Some said, "We'll hear you on this matter another time." Little did it occur to them that there would be no other time. How presumptuous of us to take for granted that there will be other opportunities available. Now is the acceptable time. And some very few believed: Dionysius, who may have become the first Bishop of Athens: and a woman, Damaris, who might have been a prostitute, for respectable women would not be in the marketplace with men.

Why did Paul fail? He has used a philosophical approach to the faith. He would never do this again. In his first letter to the Corinthians (1:17-25), he expressed how he felt about this kind of presentation. Of course, the intellectual pride of his hearers played a great part in his failure (1Cor. 2:1-5). Intellectual pride is always one of the greatest obstacles to the faith.

Paul in Corinth (18:1-11). After this failure, Paul trekked to Corinth. Corinth was the key city of Greece. Greece was almost cut in two by the sea. An isthmus, a small neck of land, less than five miles wide, connected the north of Greece with the south. On this isthmus stood the city of Corinth. The city had two seaports;

that of Lechaion for ships from the west and that of Cenchreae for ships from the east.

Besides standing between the north and south of Greece, Corinth was also the center for traffic east and west. To sail around the south of Greece, Cape Malea, was as perilous as sailing around Cape Horn. So men dragged their ships from port to port, from Lechaion to Cenchreae and back.

In consequence, Corinth was a great commercial center. Its inhabitants were traders, not manufacturers; they were engaged in getting money, not in producing things. Mere money-making is neither elevating, refining nor morally bracing. Being a trading center, it drew men of all nationalities and kinds. Corinth was pleasure mad; so often pleasure is the natural outlet for those enslaved by money. The temple of Aphrodite was there and had 1,000 priestess dedicated to sacred prostitution. At night they went into the city to ply their trade. Thus the word "Corinthian" meant a drunkard or a prostitute.

Corinth was Sin City., Yet it was here that Paul won some of his greatest triumphs. He found that sins of the flesh are far less an obstacle to the faith than the intellectual pride of the Athenians.

When Paul reached Corinth, he was a broken man. All his oratorical abilities had failed in Athens. Persecution had dogged his steps wherever he had sown the faith. He was alone, lonesome, and without funds. So he went back to work. But he had still to face the hostility of the Jews and the depravity of the city.

Yet things did change. He met two wonderful friends, who were already Christians: a Jew, Aquila, and his wife, Priscilla. There were refugees in Corinth because of the edict of Claudius banishing all Jews from Rome in 49-50 A.D. Very likely, they had been converts of St. Peter.

Paul stayed with his new found friends and worked with them, for they too were tentmakers. Friends and work are the best remedies for discouragement. Then every Sabbath, Paul entered the synagogue and tried to convince Jew and Greeks of the gospel message. Finally, his cup of joy was full when Silas and Timothy came down from Macedonia. They brought money, so that Paul could now devote all his time to preaching (2 Cor. 11:8-9).

It was here at Corinth that Paul changed his message. Up to now, it had always been Resurrection-Parousia. From now on, it was to be Passion-Resurrection. Paul had learned that suffering accepted with love always let to conversions, to resurrections. His entire European, experience thus far had been one of persecution, yet one of success; his one failure was in Athens where he was not persecuted. So when he got to Corinth, he told the Corinthians, "I resolved to know nothing while I was with you except Jesus Christ, and him crucified." (1 Cor. 2:2).

However, we must not think of Jesus, nor of Paul, as being persons who desired the cross sadistically, as though it were an end in itself. Both sought the cross, because they saw that through it, accepted in love, the cross would lead to life.

Suppose a mother had a wayward daughter. The mother loves her tenderly. She counsels her, rebukes her, instructs her, encourages her, shows her every kind of love. But all to no avail.

Now suppose God revealed to her that the only way to save her child was to die and appear before His throne. So the mother desires death, not for itself, but in order to get to the throne and obtain the saving grace for her child.

Similarly, Jesus desired the cross, and so did Paul, for they both knew that only through the cross could all mankind come to the light of life—*per crucem ad lucem.*

Yet Paul's preaching produced different effects. That is to be expected, for the receiver controls input; the soil the fructibility of the seed. Light a match, drop it in the sand, it will go out. Drop it in a wastepaper basket, it will start a fire. Drop in into a keg of dynamite, it will cause a mighty explosion. So with the light of the truth of the gospel. The Jews opposed Paul and insulted him. The Gentiles received him. So Paul left the synagogue for a house next to it, belonging to a Gentile Titus Justus. Crispus, a leading man of the synagogue (1 Cor. 1:14), and his whole household believed and were baptized, as did many other Corinthians.

Paul must have had his moods. Who would not? If you saw a person fall overboard from a steamer into the ocean, wouldn't you raise a hue and cry? The situation deserves an outcry. A life is in grave danger. So we use sirens in ambulances and on fire trucks.

Trivial matters do not merit such attention. And that is the difference between zeal and fanaticism.

Zeal deals with great things, like eternal salvation; fanaticism makes a lot of noise about trivia, is much ado about nothing. Paul was zealous; he saw the danger of damnation to so many, so he cried out. He cared. Yet Paul's zeal had its ups and downs. He was scourged at Philippi; chased out of Thessalonica; rejected at Athens; attacked viciously in Corinth by his fellow countrymen, the Jews. It was enough to make a saint despair. The best of men are men at their best. They are human after all.

But God never abandons His own. Jesus promised to be with us all days. When He gives a job to do, He also gives the power to do it. So at this critical moment in Paul's life, when fear and discouragement threatened his apostolate, Jesus appeared at night and said, "Do not be afraid. Go on speaking, and do not be silent, for I am with you." (1 Cor. 18:8-10). If God be with us, who can be against us.

"Go on speaking," said Jesus. "No one will attack and harm you, for I have many people in this city." Apparently, Paul's great temptation was to give up preaching in Corinth. At Athens, intellectual pride made his preaching sterile. Here, the Greeks were so steeped in sensuality, talking to them was like talking to a wall. The Jews, too, were each set against having a crucified Messiah— talking to them was like waving a red flag before a bull. Paul was for giving up here.

But Jesus said, "Go on speaking, and do not be silent." And why did Jesus command this? First, "I am with you"; therefore no harm can come to you. Secondly, "I have many people in this city."

One day in walking through the streets of Florence, Michaelangelo saw a cast away piece of marble, covered with dirt and filth. He retrieved it, cleaned it. Friends asked why he did this. Michaelangelo answered, "There's an angel in that block and I am going to make him visible." So Jesus saw among the Corinthians, besmirched and defiled by sin, angels and saints. And He was asking Paul to make them visible.

Too often the good think that they are fewer than they are. I remember once that Douglas Hyde, a convert from Communism, told us that the strategy of the Communist is to get people thinking that everybody is on their side, when in reality they are a small minority. Thus people will give up. Elijah thought he was the only one standing up to Jezebel. God told him there were 7,000 men who had not bowed the knee to Baal (1 King 19:18). More people are on God's side than we may realize.

That was all Paul needed. He settled down in Corinth for a year and a half and taught the word of God among the people. During this stay (51-53 A.D.), he wrote his *two Letters to the Thessalonians.*

Accusations before Gallio (18:12-17). Gallio was the older brother of Seneca. He was proconsul of Achaia in 51-52 A.D. He was kind, fair and impartial. Being mild and new at the job, the Jews thought they could manipulate him.

They brought Paul before him and began to accuse him of breaking the Mosaic law. Before Paul could answer, Gallio cut him short. For defense was unnecessary, since no Roman law had been broken. So Gallio brusquely dismissed the case.

How sad for Gallio that he did not let Paul speak. He might have been converted. But today we remember him, like Pilate, only because of his brush with Christianity. Gallio had considered Paul's religion beneath his notice. Ralph Waldo Emerson studied all religions except Christian religion, because he had jumped to the conclusion that Christianity had nothing to offer him. The danger for modern man is to think religion does not matter. Rightly Jesus taught us to pray, "Lead us not into temptation"—the temptation of thinking we don't need God!

Having failed before Gallio, the Jews ventilated their fury on Sosthenes, the synagogue official, and beat him in full view of the tribunal. But Gallio did nothing.

Paul felt he had a right now to stay in Corinth. After a year and a half, he took leave quietly—the first time he did not have to flee at night or for his life. He left with Aquila and Priscilla for the port of Cenchreae. There, he shaved his head because of a vow he had taken. The vow was perhaps in thanksgiving to God for having delivered him from the dangers and fears that had enveloped him at Corinth. The shorn hair was kept to be burned at the altar in the Temple of Jerusalem. The fact he took such a vow (Number 6:1-

21) should have made it clear to the Jews that he did not despise all their laws. (1 Cor. 9:20-23).

Aquila and Priscilla accompanied Paul only as far as Ephesus, probably for business reasons. Paul promised to come back, "God willing" (*Deo volente*). He went on to Caesarea, then on to Jerusalem to fulfill the rest of his vow, namely, to burn his hair. From there he went back to his home base at Syrian Antioch about 53 A.D.

Thus ended Paul's second missionary journey. From it he learned that God, not man, charts the course of the Church.

Acts 18:24 - 19:40

Apollos [24] A Jew named Apollos, a native of Alexandria, an eloquent speaker, arrived in Ephesus. He was an authority on the scriptures. [25] He had been instructed in the Way of the Lord and, with ardent spirit, spoke and taught accurately about Jesus, although he knew only the baptism of John. [26] He began to speak boldly in the synagogue; but when Priscilla and Aquila heard him, they took him aside and explained to him the Way [of God] more accurately. [27] And when he wanted to cross to Achaia, the brothers encouraged him and wrote to the disciples there to welcome him. After his arrival he gave great assistance to those who had come to believe through grace. [28] He vigorously refuted the Jews in public, establishing from the scriptures that the Messiah is Jesus.

19 Paul in Ephesus [1] While Apollos was in Corinth, Paul traveled through the interior of the country and came [down] to Ephesus where he found some disciples. [2] He said to them, "Did you receive the Holy Spirit when you became believer?" They answered him, "We have never even heard that there is a Holy Spirit." [3] He said, "How were you baptized?" They replied, "With the baptism of John." [4] Paul then said, "John baptized with a baptism of repentance, telling the people to believe in the one who was to come after him, that is, in Jesus." [5] When they heard this, they were baptized in the name of the Lord Jesus." [6] And when *Paul laid [his] hands on them, the Holy Spirit came upon them* and they spoke in tongues and prophesied. [7] Altogether there were about twelve men.

[8] He entered the synagogue, and for three months debated boldly with persuasive arguments about the kingdom of God. [9] But when some in their obstinacy and disbelief disparaged the Way before the assembly, he withdrew and took his disciples with him and began to hold daily discussion *in the lecture hall of Tyrannus.* [10] This continued for *two years* with the result that all the inhabitants of the province of Asia heard the works of the Lord, Jews and Greeks

alike. [11] So extraordinary were the mighty deeds God accomplished at the hands of Paul [12] that when face cloths or aprons that touched his skin were applied to the sick, their diseases left them and the evil spirits came out of them.

The Jewish Exorcists [13] Then some itinerant Jewish exorcists tried to invoke the name of the Lord Jesus over those with evil spirits, saying, "I adjure you by the Jesus whom Paul preaches." [14] When the seven sons of Sceva, a Jewish high priest, tried to do this, [15] the evil spirit said to them in reply, "Jesus I recognize, Paul I know, but who are you?" [16] The person with the evil spirit then sprang at them and subdued them all. He so overpowered them that they fled naked and wounded from that house. [17] When this became known to all the Jews and Greeks who lived in Ephesus, fear fell upon them all, and the *name of the Lord Jesus was held in great esteem.* [18] Many of those who had become believers came forward and openly acknowledged their former practices. [19] Moreover, a large number of those who had practiced magic collected their *books and burned them in public.* They calculated their value and found it to be fifty thousand silver pieces. [20] Thus did the word of the Lord continue to spread with influence and power.

Paul's Plans [21] When this was concluded, Paul made up his mind to travel through Macedonia and Achaia, and then to go on to Jerusalem, saying, "After I have been there, I might visit Rome also." [22] Then he sent to Macedonia two of his assistants, *Timothy* and *Erastus*, while he himself stayed for a while in the province of Asia.

The Riot of the Silversmiths [23] About that time a serious disturbance broke out concerning the Way. [24] There was a silversmith named *Demetrius* who made miniature silver shrines of Artemus and provided no little work for the craftsmen. [25] He called a meeting of these and other workers in related crafts and said, "Men, you know well that our prosperity derives from this work. [26] As you can now see and hear, not only in Ephesus but throughout most of the province of Asia this Paul has persuaded and mislead a great number of people by saying that gods made by hands are not gods at all. [27] The danger grows, not only that our business will be discredited, but also that the temple of the great goddess Artemis will be of no account, and that she whom the whole province of Asia and all the world worship will be stripped of her magnificence."

[28] When they heard this, they were filled with fury and began to shout. "Great is Artemis of the Ephesians!" [29] The city was filled with confusion, and the people rushed with one accord into the theater, seizing *Gaius* and *Aristarchus*, the Macedonians, *Paul's traveling companions*. [30] Paul wanted to go before the crowd, but the disciples would not let him. [31] and even some of the Asiarchs who were friends of his sent work to him advising him not to venture into the theater. [32] Meanwhile, some were shouting one thing, others something else; the assembly was in chaos, and most of the people had no idea why they had come together. [33] Some of the crowd prompted *Alexander*, as the Jews pushed him forward, and Alexander signaled with his hand that he wished to explain something to the gathering. [34] But when they recognized that he was a Jew, they all shouted in unison, for about *two hours*, "Great is Artemis of the Ephesians!" [35] Finally the *town clerk* restrained the crowd and said, "You Ephesians, what person is there who does not know that the city of the Ephesians is the guardian of the temple of the great Artemis and of her image that fell from the sky? [36] Since these things are undeniable, you must calm yourselves and not do anything rash. [37] The men you brought here are not temple robbers, nor have they insulted our goddess. [38] If Demetrius and his fellow craftsmen have a complaint against anyone, courts are in session, and there are proconsuls. Let them bring charges against one another. [39] If you have anything further to investigate, let the matter be settled in the lawful assembly, [40] for, as it is, we are in danger of being charged with rioting because of today's conduct. There is no cause for it. We shall [not] be able to give a reason for this demonstration." With these words he dismissed the assembly.

Acts 20: 1-38

20 Journey to Macedonia and Greece [1] When the disturbance was over, Paul had the disciples summoned and, after encouraging them, he bade them farewell and set out on
his journey to Macedonia. [2] As he traveled throughout those
regions, he provided many words of encouragement for
them. Then he arrived in Greece [3] where he stayed for three
months. But when a plot was made against him by the Jews
as he was about to set sail for Syria, he decided to return by
way of Macedonia.

Return to Troas [4] Sopater, the son of Pyrrhus, from
Beroea, accompanied him, as did Aristarchus and Secundus
from Thessalonica, Gaius from Derbe, Timothy, and
Tychicus and Trophimus from Asia [5] who went on ahead
and waited for us at Troas. [6] We sailed from Philippi after
the feast of Unleavened Bread, and rejoined them five days
later in Troas, where we spent a week.

Eutychus Restored to Life [7] On the first day of the
week when we gathered to break bread, Paul spoke to them
because he was going to leave on the next day, and he kept
on speaking until midnight. [8] There were many lamps in the
upstairs room where we were gathered, [9] and a young man
named Eutychus who was sitting on the window sill was
sinking into a deep sleep as Paul talked on and on. Once
overcome by sleep he fell down from the third story and
when he was picked up, *he was dead.* [10] *Paul went down,*
threw himself upon him, and said as he embraced him.
"Don't be alarmed; there is life in him." [11] Then he returned
upstairs, broke the bread, and ate; after a long conversation
that lasted until daybreak, he departed. [12] And they took the
boy away alive and were immeasurably comforted.

Journey to Miletus [13] We went ahead to the ship and
set sail for Assos where we were to take Paul on board, as
he had arranged, since he was going overland. [14] When he
met us in Assos, we took him aboard and went on to
Mitylene. [15] We sailed away from there on the next day and
reached a point off Chios, and a day later we reached Samos,

and on the following day we arrived at Miletus. [16] Paul had decided to sail past Ephesus in order not to lose time in the province of Asia, for he was hurrying to be in Jerusalem, if at all possible, for the day of Pentecost.

Paul's Farewell Speech at Miletus [17] From Miletus he had the presbyters of the church at Ephesus summoned. [18] When they came to him, he addressed them, "You know how I lived among you the whole time from the day I first came to the province of Asia. [19] *I served the Lord with all humility* and with the tears and trials that came to me because of the plots of the Jews, [20] and I did not at all shrink from telling you what was for your benefit, or from teaching you in public or in your homes. [21] I earnestly *bore witness* for both Jews and Greeks to repentance before God and to faith in our Lord Jesus. [22] But now, compelled by the Spirit, I am going to Jerusalem. What will happen to me there I do not know, [23] except that in one city after another the Holy Spirit has been warning me that imprisonment and hardships await me. [24] Yet I consider life of no importance to men, if only I may finish my course and the ministry that I received from the Lord Jesus, to bear witness to the gospel of God's grace.

[25] "But now I know that none of you to whom I preached the kingdom during my travels will ever see my face again. [26] And so I solemnly declare to you this day that I am not responsible for the blood of any of you, [27] for I did not shrink from proclaiming to you the entire plan of God. [28] *Keep watch* over yourselves and over the whole flock of which the Holy Spirit has appointed you overseers, in which you tend the church of God that he acquired with his own blood. [29] I know that after my departure savage wolves will come among you, and they will not spare the flock. [30] And from your own group, men will come forward perverting the truth to draw the disciples away after them [31] So be vigilant and remember that for three years, night and day, I unceasingly admonished each of you with tears. [32] And now I commend you to God and to that gracious word of his that can build you up and give you the inheritance among all who are con-

secrated. [33] I have *never wanted anyone's* silver or gold or clothing. [34] You know well that these very hands have served my needs and my companions. [35] In every way I have shown you that by hard work of that sort we must help the weak, and keep in mind the words of the Lord Jesus who himself said, 'It is more blessed to give than to receive.'"

[36] When he had finished speaking he knelt down and prayed with them all. [37] They were all weeping loudly as they threw their arms around Paul and kissed him, [38] for they were deeply distressed that he had said that they would never see his face again. Then they escorted him to the ship.

Acts 21: 1-14

21 Arrival at Tyre [1] When we had taken leave of them we set sail, made a straighter run for Cos, and on the next day for Rhodes, and from there to Patara. [2] Finding a ship crossing to Phoenicia, we went on board and put out to sea. [3] We caught sight of Cyprus but passed by it on our left and sailed on toward Syria and put in at Tyre where the ship was to unload cargo. [4] There we sought out the disciples and stayed for a week. They kept telling Paul through the Spirit not to embark for Jerusalem. [5] At the end of our stay we left and resumed our journey. All of them, women and children included, escorted us out of the city, and after kneeling on the beach to pray [6] we bade farewell to one another. Then we boarded the ship, and they returned home.

Arrival at Ptolemais and Caesarea [7] We continued the voyage and came from Tyre to Ptolemais, where we greeted the brothers and stayed a day with them. [8] On the next day we resumed the trip and came to Caesarea, where we went to the house of Philip the evangelist, who was one of the Seven, and stayed with him. [9] He had four virgin daughters gifted with prophecy. [10] We had been there several days when a prophet named Agabus came down from Judea. [11] He came up to us, took Paul's belt, bound his own feet and hands with it, and said. "Thus says the Holy Spirit: This is the way the Jews will bind the owner of this belt in

Jerusalem, and they will hand him over to the Gentiles." [12] When we heard this, we and the local residents begged him not to go up to Jerusalem. [13] Then Paul replied, "What are you doing, weeping and breaking my heart? I am prepared not only to be bound but even to die in Jerusalem for the name of the Lord Jesus." [14] Since he would not be dissuaded we let the matter rest, saying. "The Lord's will be done."

Facts on Acts

CHAPTER 13

Paul's Third Missionary Journey 54-59 A.D.

2800 miles

(*Acts* 18:24-21:14)

Luke glides almost imperceptibly into Paul's third missionary journey. Nothing is said about who accompanied him. But Paul seldom traveled along. Probably Timothy was with him. They traveled through the Galatian country and Phrygia. No doubt they revisited Derbe and Lystra, Timothy's hometown. This would have been his third visit to the Lycaonian cities and his second to Galatia and Phyrgia.

While Paul was strengthening the churches in this area, Luke tells us what was going on in Ephesus.

Appollos (18:24-28). Appollos was a native of Alexandria in Egypt. Alexandria was a city of learning, famous for its library. About a million Jews lived there. Here the Hebrew Scriptures were translated into Greek, a translation known as the Septuagint. Here, side by side, with schools of Greek philosophy, there arose a famous school of biblical interpretation, an allegorical interpretation of the Bible, in which each Old Testament event was supposed to have another hidden meaning.

Appollos was an eloquent speaker and an authority on the Scriptures. He was full of zeal, knew about the baptism of John, but very little about Jesus. He had come by boat to Ephesus.

155

**PAUL'S THIRD
MISSIONARY JOURNEY**
Acts 18:23-21:17 (54-58 A.D.)
about 2800 miles

Aquila and Priscilla had been left in Ephesus by Paul. Since no Christian community existed there at the time, they attended the synagogue services. One Sabbath, Apollos came to this same synagogue. He was invited to speak. He spoke eloquently and earnestly on what he knew about Jesus—but that was very little. Aquila and Priscilla saw his sincerity and also his lack of knowledge. So they brought him to their home and explained to him God's new way in greater detail. The commonest designation of Christianity in Acts is "The Way," The term implied that *Christianity is a way of life and living, not just a creed* — but a faith that issues in works.

Apollos was humble enough to learn from the two tentmakers. He wanted to sail over to Corinth. The brothers encouraged this and wrote to the disciples there to welcome him. At Corinth, he proved to be a great help to the Christians there, for he vigorously refuted the Jews and proved from Scriptures that Jesus was the Messiah. Apollos became so popular there that a party was formed, calling themselves followers of Apollos. Apollos seemed to have resented this, for he declined to return to Corinth later (1 Cor. 16:12).

Paul in Ephesus (19:1-12). After Apollos had left for Corinth, Paul came to Ephesus. He discovered that the disciples there were at the same religious level that Apollos had been. They had never heard of the Holy Spirit and were baptized only with the baptism of John. After Paul had explained that John's baptism was for repentance and a preparation for Jesus, they believed and were baptized in the name of the Lord. Paul then confirmed them and the Holy Spirit came upon them and they spoke in tongues and prophesied. It was a repeat of the Jewish Pentecost for the Greeks.

Paul probably lodged with Aquil and Priscilla again. For three months, he went to the synagogue and debated boldly about the kingdom of God. But when some in their obstinacy and disbelief disparaged him, he left and took his disciples with him and established his own meeting place in the lecture hall of Tyrannus. This man was probably a converted Jewish physician, known to Luke. An unconverted pagan philosopher would hardly have lent his classroom to a preacher of a new faith.

Paul's teaching day was from 11:00 A.M. to 4:00 P.M. In Ionian cities, eleven to four o'clock was siesta time. More people were asleep at 1:00 P.M. in Ephesus than at 1:00 A.M. Paul worked at his trade until 11:00 A.M. during the siesta hours, he taught and handled his correspondence. *The First Letter to the Corinthians* was written at this time.

Paul stayed in Ephesus longer than anywhere else, nearly three years (54-56 B.C.). He taught at Tyrannus' place daily for two years. The result was "all the inhabitants of the province of Asia heard the word of the Lord," Jews and Greeks alike. No doubt this included the seven cities mentioned in the book of Revelation (Rv. 1:11), plus Colossae and Hierapolis, which were probably evangelized by Epaphras (Col. 1:7). Paul's other co-workers were Timothy, Erastus, Gaius and Aristarchus.

Ephesus was the seat of magical arts. Sorcerers used scrolls and rhymes against calamity and to prevent pregnancies. (The word "sorcery" comes from the Greek work, *pharmakeia,* our pharmacy. Sorcerers used drugs to prevent birth of children. Hence it was strongly condemned, (Gal. 5:20; Rv. 9:21). So God worked mighty deeds at the hands of Paul-no incantations were needed, not even his presence: the mere touch of his handkerchief or a cloth which had touched his skin healed the sick and drove out demons. (Here we have a precedent for third class relics in the Church.).

The Jewish Exorcists (19:13-20). Healing with cloths touched to Paul's skin might have looked like magic to the Ephesians. Luke shows it was not narrating the incident of the Jewish exorcists who tried to use the name of Jesus magically.

Magic would be to use the name of Jesus, without following Him, as Paul did. The exorcists did not say, "I adjure you by the Jesus we love." No, they said, "I adjure you by the Jesus, Paul preaches." Exorcists today are of the same ilk, who try to do good in the name of Christianity, but do not try to be good Christians. The effect of using the name of Jesus magically was ludicrous, almost humorous. The evil spirit stripping the exorcists naked, beating the, and making them run helter-skelter for their lives reads like slapstick comedy.

But the crowd's reaction showed that the people got their point. Their awe and reverence for the name of Jesus and for Paul increased. They repented by burning their books of magic in a public bonfire. Too often one hates sin, but does not leave it. Here a clean break was made. They didn't even ask how will we earn a living from now on.

The pen is mightier than the sword. The printing press is the mightiest agency in the world for good or for evil. Time is short; therefore, we have time, not just for good books, but only for the best. David Hume and Voltaire became agnostics through bad reading in their youth. St. Augustine, St. Francis of Assisi, the Little Flower of Jesus, St. Therese—all were transformed into saints by verses from Scriptures.

A person who carries gunpowder should not get too close to the fire. Therefore avoid books that give a false picture of life, that inflame passion, that give a false morality—condone crimes, immorality. It was bad books that stirred up Alexander Serenelli to try to rape St. Maria Goretti; when he failed, he killed her.

Paul's Plans (19:21-22). This note about Paul's future plans is put here before the riot of the silversmiths to make it clear that he was not frightened by that event to leave Ephesus. He had already made up his mind to travel through Macedonia (Philippi and Thessalonica) and Achaia (Corinth) and from there to go on to Jerusalem.

Then he said, "I must visit Rome"—no ifs or ands, but "I must." Aquila and Priscilla knew Rome first hand. No doubt they had told Paul of the strong Christianity there, of the mighty city with its influx of strangers, with the freedom a great capital always affords for the dissemination of new ideas—all of which determined Paul to want to go.

He sent two of his assistants, Timothy and Erastus, to Macedonia (c. 56 A.D.), ahead of himself. He wanted them to take up a relief collection for the church in Jerusalem and to bring to the Corinthians his *First Letter* (1 Cor. 16:1-9), appealing for unity in their community.

The Riot of the Silversmiths (19:23-40). About this time a serious disturbance broke out concerning the Way. Again the term "the Way" is used for the teaching of the apostles, for they constantly insisted in their preaching that Christ was "the way" to salvation. The story is told as the climax of Paul's stay in Ephesus. It shows how the forces of evil were terrified, baffled and defeated. The very institution of idolatry seemed to be tottering right at its very center.

The instigator of the opposition was a silversmith Demetrius. Like many others, he tried to cover up his greed under the cloak of religious zeal and love for the goddess, Artemis. The most sensitive part of worldly men is their pocketbooks. How often criticism of the Church is really for economic, not spiritual reasons!

Anyway, Demetrius declared his concern over the honor due to Artemis, the moon goddess. At Ephesus she was worshipped as an Asian mother goddess of fertility. She was one of the most widely worshipped female deities in the Greek world. Her temple at Ephesus was one of the seven wonders of the ancient world. The silversmiths there made miniature silver shrines of Artemis and sold them to the large numbers of pilgrims coming there to worship the goddess. They would take these home as souvenirs of their visit. But Christianity had made such strides that this trade of theirs was seriously threatened.

The crowd responded "Great is Artemis of the Ephesians!" In 431 A.D. in this very city of Ephesus, the Council of Ephesus would declare Mary to be the Mother of God (the *Theotokos*). And the people would carry the Bishops of the Council through the streets, chanting "Mary, *Theotokos*" — "Mary, the God-bearer."

But in Paul's day, a near riot broke out. The people seized Gaius and Aristarchus, Paul's Macedonian traveling companions, and brought them to the theater. Paul, fearless as always, wanted to go before the crowd and speak to them, but his disciples thought this unwise. There was confusion in the assembly. Alexander tried to bring order, but to no avail. The crowd kept chanting for two hours, "Great is Artemis of the Ephesians!"

Finally, the town clerk intervened. He was worried about his job. One thing Rome did not tolerate was public disorder. Should such a thing happen, Rome would know why and the magistrates responsible for keeping order would lose their jobs. The town clerk agreed that Ephesus was the guardian of the great temple of Artemis and "of her image that fell from the sky." The image was probably a meteorite that fell from the sky and was encased in the image of Artemis. He succeeded in quieting the mob, and he dismissed them.

Journey to Macedonia and Greece (20:1-3). When the disturbance was over, Paul summoned the disciples to say good-bye to them before setting out for Macedonia, a journey he had planned before the riot. He certainly revisited Philippi, Thessalonica, and Beroea (c. 57 A.D.) Perhaps from Macedonia, Paul wrote his *Second Letter to the Corinthians* and his *Letter to the Galatians.*

From Macedonia he went on to Greece, to Corinth, where he stayed for three months. And from there he wrote his *Letter to the Romans.*

When he was about to sail for Syria, he learned of a plot of the Jews to throw him overboard. The Jews were shrewd traders; therefore they were numerous in seaport towns, like Cenchreae, and so could easily have done harm to Paul. Therefore, Paul abandoned the sea voyage for the long, but safer, journey by land through Macedonia, where there were fewer Jews. This longer journey caused him to miss the Passover in Jerusalem. However, he hoped to get there for Pentecost.

Return to Troas (20:4-6). Paul was accompanied by seven men, representative of all the places he had evangelized. These men were probably delegates from the various churches, charged with bringing their relief collections to the Church in Jerusalem. These went on ahead and waited for Paul at Troas. At Philippi, Paul probably stayed at the house of Lydia for the Passover feast; then he and Luke sailed for Troas, where they spent a week.

Eutyches Restored to Life (20:7-12). At Troas "on the first day of the week when we gathered to break bread, Paul spoke...until midnight." This is the oldest witness to Mass on Sunday in the New Testament (cp., Rv.1:10). Luke mentions it so casually that the inference is, the early Christians usually celebrated Mass on Sunday.

Services were at night, because so many of the Christians were slaves or laborers who had to work during the day. Probably Eutyches was one of these. He was dead tired. He probably sat in a window to get the cool night air and keep awake. But the stuffy atmosphere and the fumes from the many lamps in the upstairs room put him sound to sleep. He fell out of the third story window. Luke said he was dead. Paul restored him to life. Eutyches is the Greek word for "lucky." (Moral; don't sleep during sermons, you'll die spiritually.

Journey to Miletus (20:13-16). When Paul left Troas, his companion went by boat to Assos (30 miles by sea) while Paul walked there by land (20 miles). Paul wanted it that way, because he wanted to be alone. We need solitude, we need exercise, so Paul walked alone to Assos. There, he rejoined his companions, boarded ship and sailed for Mitylene. The next day they went on to Chios and Samos and stopped at Miletus (28 miles south west of Ephesus, for a few days.

Paul's Farewell Speech at Miletus (20:17:38). Luke parallels Paul's life here with Jesus. As Jesus felt compelled to go to Jerusalem for His last Passover, so did Paul feel the same compulsion. At the Last Supper Jesus gave a farewell address, so Paul did the same here.

"From Miletus he had the presbyters of the Church at Ephesus summoned..." Authorities in Jewish communities were called presbyters; so it was natural for them to adopt the same title for their religious leaders. However in verse 28, the presbyters are called overseers (*episkopoi*)

In Paul's time the terms presbyters (elders) and overseers (*episkopoi*) were interchangeable. Presbyters probably stressed dignity; overseers may have accented function. Not until the end of the first century was presbyter used to designate priests and overseer to mean bishops, as we know them today. Thus St. Ignatius (+107 A.D.). in his Letter to the Ephesians wrote: "Your excellent presbyters, who are a credit to God, are as suited to the bishop as string to a harp." In his letter to the Trallians, he wrote: "...all should respect the deacons as Jesus Christ, just as all should regard the Bishop as the image of the Father, and the clergy as God's senate and the college of the apostles. Without these three orders you cannot begin to speak of a church."

This farewell address reveals the heart of Paul. To the presbyters, he set himself up as an example. He reviewed the *past*: "I served the Lord with all humility; I suffered, but I did not shrink from doing my duty—preaching, teaching and witnessing."

Then he spoke of the *present*: of how the Holy Spirit was driving him toward Jerusalem, just as the Spirit had caused Jesus to "set his face steadfast like flint toward Jerusalem" (Lk. 9:51). Though the Spirit made it clear to Paul by interior inspirations and exterior revelation that affliction awaited him in Jerusalem, still Paul went on fearlessly.

Then Paul looked into the *future*: he warned the elders that the Church would be persecuted from without — "savage wolves will come among you": and persecuted from within — "and from your own group, men will come forward perverting the truth." Paul knew this from experience, because these same things happened in every church he had founded when he left. So he alerted them: "Keep watch. Be vigilant— just as I was." Then he urged them to work, just as he had often done, in order to become financially independent of their flock and also to be able to help the poor among them. He concluded by quoting the words of the Lord: "It is more blessed to give than to receive."

This scene is proof of Paul's ability to make personal and lasting friendships. They all wept loudly, threw their arms around Paul and kissed him. They sorrowed most, because he had told them, "they would never see his face again. Then they escorted him to the ship."

Arrival at Tyre and Caesarea (21:1-14). Paul's journey from Miletus to Jerusalem was a fast one. They made a straight run for Cos; then on the next day for the isle of Rhodes: and from there, to Patara. "Finding a ship crossing to Phoenicia, we went on board and put out to sea. We caught sight of Cyprus but passed by it on our left and sailed on toward Syria and put in at Tyre."

At Tyre they stayed seven days. One day at Ptolemais; a few days with Philip at Caesarea; then Jerusalem.

This travelogue brings out two great facts about Paul: the deep affection in which he was held by his friends; and his matchless courage — "I am prepared...even to die in Jerusalem for the name of the Lord Jesus." As he approached Jerusalem. the presentiment at Miletus becomes clearer, and the warning more insistent. So his friends, acting like Peter who had tried to dissuade Christ from His passion and death, tried to deter Paul from going to Jerusalem.

The incident with the prophet Agabus showed that Paul, in going to Jerusalem, was acting, not contrary to the Holy Spirit, as some had claimed, but in accord with the dictates of the Holy Spirit. God willed that the path to Rome be through Jerusalem. God willed that the Jews have one last chance to hear the gospel from one who loved them, who had been one of their leaders, who came bearing collections from the other churches as proof of that love. Their rejection sealed their fate and resulted in the sending of the gospel to Rome and the Gentile world.

Acts 21:15-23:11

Paul and James in Jerusalem [15] After these days we made preparation for our journey, then went up to Jerusalem. [16] Some of the disciples from Caesarea came along to lead us to the house of Mnason, a Cypriot, a disciple of long standing, with whom we were to stay. [17] When we reached Jerusalem the brothers welcomed us warmly. [18] The next day, Paul accompanied us on a visit to James, and all the presbyters were present. [19] He greeted them, then proceeded to tell them in detail what God had accomplished among the Gentiles through his ministry. [20] They praised God when they heard it but said to him, "Brother, you see how many thousands of believers there are from among the Jews, and they are all zealous believers of the law. [21] They have been informed that you are teaching all the Jews who live among the Gentiles to abandon Moses and that you are telling them not to circumcise their *children or to observe* their customary practices. [22] What is to be done? They will surely hear that you have arrived. [23] So do what we tell you. We have four men who have taken a vow. [24] Take these men and purify yourself with them, and pay their expenses that they may have their heads shaved. In this way everyone will know that there is nothing to the reports they have been given about you but that you yourself live in observance of the law. [25] As for the Gentiles who have come to believe, we sent them our decision that they abstain from meat sacrificed to idols, from blood, from the meat of strangled animals, and from unlawful marriage. [26] So Paul took the men and on the next day after purifying himself together with them entered the temple to give notice of the day when the purification would be completed and the offering made for each of them.

Paul's arrest [27] When the seven days were nearly completed, the Jews from the province of Asia noticed him in the temple, stirred up the whole crowd, and laid hands on him, [28] shouting, "Fellow Israelites, help us. This is the man who is teaching everyone everywhere against the people and the law and this place, and what is more, he has even brought Greeks into the temple and defiled this sacred place." [29] For they had previously seen Trophimus the Ephesian in the city with him and supposed that Paul had brought him into the temple. [30] The whole city was in turmoil with people rushing together. They seized Paul and dragged him out of the temple, and immediately the gates were closed. [31] While they were trying to kill him, a report reached the cohort commander that *all Jerusalem was rioting*. [32] He *immediately* took soldier and centurions and charged down on them. When they saw the commander and the soldiers they stopped beating Paul. [33] The cohort commander came forward, arrested him and ordered him to be secured with two chains; he tried to find out who he might be and what he had done. [34] Some in the mob shouted one thing, others something else; so, since he was unable to ascertain the truth because of the uproar, he ordered Paul to be brought into the compound. [35] When he reached the steps , he was carried by the soldiers because of the violence of the mob, [36] for a crowd of people followed and shouted, "Away with him!"

[37] Just as Paul was about to be taken into the compound, he said to the cohort commander, "May I say something to you?" He replied, "Do you speak Greek? [38] So then you are not the Egyptian who started a revolt some time ago and let the four thousand assassins into the desert?"[39] Paul answered, "I am a Jew, of Tarsus in Cicilia, a citizen of no mean city; I request you to permit me to speak to the people." [40] When he had given his permission, Paul stood on the steps and motioned with his hand to the people; and when all was quiet he addressed then in Hebrew.

22 Paul's Defense before the Jerusalem Jews [1] "My brothers and fathers, listen to what I am about to say to you in my defense." [2] When they heard him addressing them in Hebrew they became all the more quiet. And he continued, [3] "I am a Jew, born in Tarsus in Cilicia, but brought up in this city. At the feet of Gamaliel I was educated strictly in our ancestral law and was zealous for God, just as all of you are today. [4] I persecuted this Way to death, binding both men and women and delivering them to prison. [5] Even the high priest and the whole council of elders can testify on my behalf. For from them I even received letters to the brothers and set out for Damascus to bring back to Jerusalem in chains for punishment those there as well.

[6] "On that journey as I drew near to Damascus, about noon a great light from the sky suddenly shone around me. [7] I fell to the ground and heard a voice saying to me. *"Saul, Saul, why are you persecuting me?"* [8] I replied, "Who are you, sir?" And he said to me, 'I am Jesus the Nazorean whom you are persecuting.' [9] My companions saw the light but did not hear the voice of the one who spoke to me. [10] I asked, *'What shall I do, sir?'* The Lord answered me, 'Get up and go into Damascus, and there *you will be told about everything appointed for you to do.'* [11] Since I could see nothing because of the brightness of that light, I was led by hand by my companions and entered Damascus.

[12] "A certain Ananias, a devout observer of the law, and highly spoken of by all the Jews who lived there, [13] came to me and stood there and said, 'Saul, my brother, regain your sight.' And at that very moment I regained my sight and saw him. [14] Then he said, 'The God of our ancestors designated you to know his will, to see the Righteous One, and to hear the sound of his voice' [15] for you will be his witness before all to what you have seen and heard. [16] Now, why delay? Get up and have yourself baptized and your sins washed away, calling upon his name.'

[17] "After I had returned to Jerusalem and while I was praying in the temple, I fell into a trance [18] and saw the Lord saying to me, 'Hurry, leave Jerusalem at once, because they will not accept your testimony about me.' [19] But I replied, 'Lord they themselves know that from synagogue to synagogue I used to imprison and beat those who believed in you. [20] And when the blood of your witness Stephen was being shed, I myself stood by giving my approval and keeping guard over the cloaks of his murderers.' [21] Then he said to me, 'Go, I shall send you far away to the Gentiles.'"

Paul Imprisoned [22] They listened to him until he said this, but then they raised their voices and shouted, "Take such a one as this away from the earth. It is not right that he should live." [23] And as they were yelling and throwing off their cloaks and flinging dust into the air, [24] the cohort commander ordered him to be brought into the compound and gave instructions that he be interrogated under the lash to determine the reason why they were making such an outcry against him. [25] But when they had stretched him out for the whips, Paul said to the centurion on duty, "Is it lawful for you to scourge a man who is a Roman citizen and has not been tried?" [26] When the centurion heard this, he went to the cohort commander and reported it saying, "What are you going to do? This man is a Roman citizen." [27] Then the commander came and said to him, "Tell me, are you a Roman citizen?" "Yes," he answered. [28] The commander replied, "I acquired this citizenship for a large sum of money." Paul said, "But I was born one." [29] At once those who were going to interrogate him backed away from him, and the commander became alarmed when he realized that he was a Roman citizen and that he had had him bound.

Paul before the Sanhedrin [30] The next day, wishing to determine the truth about why he was being accused by the Jews, he freed him and ordered the chief priests and the whole Sanhedrin to convene. Then he brought Paul down and made him stand before them.

23 [1] Paul looked intently at the Sanhedrin and said, "My brothers, I have conducted myself with a perfectly clear conscience before God to this day." [2] The high priest Ananias ordered his attendants to strike his mouth. [3] Then Paul said to him, "God will strike you, you whitewashed wall. Do you indeed sit in judgment upon me according to the law and yet in violation of the law order me to be struck?" [4] The attendants said, "Would you revile God's high priest?" [5] Paul answered, "Brothers, I did not realize he was the high priest. For it is written, 'You shall not curse a ruler of your people.'"

⁶ Paul was aware that some were Sadducees and some Pharisees, so he called out before the Sanhedrin. "My brothers, I am a Pharisee, the son of Pharisees: [I] am on trial for hope in the resurrection of the dead." ⁷ When he said this, a dispute broke out between the Pharisees and Sadducees, and the group became divided. ⁸ For the Sadducees say that there is no resurrection or angels or spirits, while the Pharisees acknowledge all three. ⁹ A great uproar occurred, and some scribes belonging to the Pharisee party stood up and sharply argued, "We find nothing wrong with this man. Suppose a spirit or an angel has spoken to him?" ¹⁰ The dispute was so serious that the commander, afraid that Paul would be torn to pieces by them, ordered his troops to go down and rescue him from their midst and take him into the compound. ¹¹ The following night the Lord stood by him and said, "Take courage. For just as you have borne witness to my cause in Jerusalem, so you must also bear witness in Rome."

Facts on Acts

CHAPTER 14

Paul in Jerusalem

(Acts 21:15-23:11)

The rest of Acts is concerned with Paul as a prisoner for Christ. It spans the time from his arrest at Jerusalem to his release in Rome four years later. For two years, he was imprisoned in Caesarea, and in Rome for two years. [1]

Paul and James in Jerusalem (21:15-26). Paul came to Jerusalem in the year 58 A.D. to bring the collections from the Gentile churches to the Mother—Church and to fulfill his Nazarite vow. He and his companions stayed with Mnason, a Cypriote and an early disciple, perhaps one of the seventy disciples of Our Lord. Being a Cypriote, he was very likely a friend of Barnabas. Since Cyprus was notorious for its immorality, Mnason opted to stay on in the religious milieu of Jerusalem.

At Jerusalem they were warmly welcomed by the brothers. The next day, Paul visited James and all the presbyters were present. Paul greeted them all and proceeded to tell them of the wonders God had worked among the Gentiles through his twelve years of ministry. Paul highlighted the results more than the difficulties of his missions, and he did this in such a self-effacing manner that the church in Jerusalem praised God, not Paul, for all that was done.

---

[1]   Luke wrote his gospel in Caesarea (58-60) and Acts in Rome (61-63).

But then the Jerusalem church began to tell Paul of their success — "thousands of Jews had come to believe." This was an oblique criticism of Paul. The believers in Jerusalem were saying, we have converted thousands without having them reject Moses and his laws. Slanderous tongues had misrepresented Paul's work. Slander, like fire, destroys all it touches good or bad. Slanderers had accused Paul of teaching that Jews living among the Gentiles could abandon Moses and his dietary and ceremonial laws—the persistent thorn in Paul's side.

He was told, perhaps for the first time, that the Council of Jerusalem had exempted Gentiles from these laws, except the dietary one of eating only kosher meats (so that they could celebrate the Eucharist together) and of abstaining from unlawful marriages. It did not become clear, however, that the Council decrees applied also to Jewish Christians, and not just to the Gentiles, until after the destruction of Jerusalem (70 A.D.).

Paul answered the charge by action, rather than by word. No principles were involved, so Paul yielded the point to keep peace. He stooped to conquer. He became a Jew to the Jews that he might gain the Jews.

Paul's Arrest (21:27-40). So he went to the Temple to discharge his vow like any true Jew. When the 7-day of purification was nearly finished, some Asian Jews (probably from Ephesus) recognized Paul. They knew of Paul's phenomenal success in Ephesus; they had been probably worsted by Paul in debate there; now they would get their revenge.

They stirred up the Jews against him by assuming Paul had brought Greeks into the Temple. Like the sudden storms on the Lake of Galilee, a furious storm of passions, sudden and unexpected, broke out. It was stilled only by the intervention of civil authority. Force has an indispensable place in the divine economy. The Jews would have murdered Paul had not the Roman soldiers intervened. Persuasion is good, but at times there is nothing to contain the passions of men by force.

Paul was arrested, chained, and ordered to be brought into the compound. Just as he was about to be taken into the compound, he requested permission to address the mob. The centurion was amazed that Paul spoke Greek. He had thought that Paul was the Egyptian insurrectionist who had recently started a revolt on the Mount of Olives. When he discovered that Paul was a Jew of Tarsus, and so a Roman citizen, he permitted Paul to speak, hoping to get at the bottom of the riot.

Again, the fearlessness of Paul. A lesser person would have retreated in silence. Not Paul. Zeal consumed him for his own people. He did not write them off. Like a physician dealing with a deadly disease, he left no stone unturned. Indifference, opposition, violence, and threats of death only enkindled his ardor, as a wind does a mighty flame.

Paul's Defense before the Jerusalem Jews (22:1-21). This is the first of several defense speeches for Paul. These speeches were written by Luke. The beginning is stereotyped: "My brothers and fathers, listen to what I am about to say..." When the mob heard him speak in Aramaic, they became quiet.

Paul was anxious to conciliate the Jews; so he identified himself as closely as possible with them. "I am a Jew, brought up in this city," he told them. "I was educated at the feet of the great Gamaliel. I persecuted this Way to death. Now I have changed. Why? Because of some great miraculous intervention." Then Paul, for a second time, described his conversion on the road to Damascus. He said, in effect, that a vision of Christ, of the glorified Christ, which none of the other apostles had received after Easter, had transformed him. This vision, plus the miracle of Ananias, a devout Jew, restoring his sight, changed him.

In the Greek mystery religions, revelation was mainly through seeing. In the Old Testament religion, revelation was by hearing as befits an anti-iconic cult. The prophets of Israel were sent with the word of Yahweh to which obedience was due. Thus a just Israelite was one who heard the word of God and kept it, not one who contemplated God. Paul presented his meeting with God in both ways: first as a seeing, then as a hearing. He saw the *kabod* of Jahweh, the divine light shining on the face of Christ. And he heard a voice speaking to him. His companions saw the light, but did not hear the voice. The voice gave meaning to the experience. For instance, a reading can be made in Latin to a room full of people. All in the room hear the reading; only those who know Latin understand it. His companions saw the light; only Paul understood what was happening.

After he had been led into the city, and after Ananias had restored his sight and baptized him, Paul said he went to Jerusalem, perhaps to preach there. Yet while he was at prayer in the temple, he fell into a trance and saw the Lord. And the Lord said to him: "Go, I shall send you far away to the Gentiles."

Paul was saying in his defense that he could not help becoming a Christian at Damascus, so he could not help preaching to the Gentiles. His first thought had been to preach to the Jews. That was why he went to the temple to pray, but Jesus told him in a trance to go to the Gentiles. In other words, it was God's will that he preach to the Gentiles. To oppose his work was to oppose God.

Paul Imprisoned (22:22-29). The word "Gentile" was a trigger word to the Jews. Paul could have skipped the word. He was in the same situation as an abolitionist would have been speaking in a slave-market in Richmond, Virginia, before the Civil War. But Paul was truthful. He told things simply as they had happened. A skilled speaker, he put the word "Gentile" last in his defense, but like a spark in a keg of gunpowder, it started an explosion.

The mob shouted, "Kill him! Such a one has no right to live." The cohort commander, the centurion Lysias, assumed Paul was guilty and was going to extract from him by torture the cause of the uproar. Paul waited until he was away from the crowd and all was quiet to declare who he was. When the centurion learned that Paul was a Roman citizen, he backed off interrogating Paul by torture. Instead, he decided to get at the bottom of things by bringing the accusers and the accused together.

Paul before the Sanhedrin (23:1-11). So the next day, Paul was brought before the Sanhedrin. Before speaking, Paul looked intently at the Sanhedrin. He was sizing up his adversaries. He looked them squarely in the eyes, for he was no criminal, nor was he cowed. He addressed them as their equal: "My brothers..." Then he declared his innocence. The High Priest, Ananias ordered his attendants to strike him on the mouth, a blow similar to that given to Jesus (Jn. 18:19-24).

Why did he order this? Did Paul's look provoke the High Priest? Or his words? Not likely. His look was one of conscious innocence and searching observation. His words were geared more to conciliate than to exasperate. Very likely, the blow was meant to silence Paul or intimidate him.

However, it was not successful. Paul blasted Ananias: "You whitewashed wall!" Ananias was High Priest from 47 to 59 A.D. Josephus says that he was cruel, dissolute, gluttonous, and avaricious. He was assassinated in 66 A.D.

Paul was rebuked for insulting God's High Priest. Paul apologized, because he did not know that Ananias held this office. At this time, the High Priesthood was a political plum juggled by the Romans and the Herods. Also, if Paul had eye trouble, he could have seen only a blurred figure in white, uttering an injustice. Such injustice was so out of character for a High Priest that the strict Pharisee Paul did not believe that a High Priest would be guilty of breaking the Law.

Seeing that his audience was composed of Sadducees and Pharisees, Paul cleverly divided them by bringing up the issue of the resurrection of the dead. That, or course, was not the issue; the issue was that *Paul was undermining Judaism by going to the Gentiles.* However, Paul saw he could get no justice here, so it was good sense to draw support from wherever he could. The Sadducees denied the resurrection; the Pharisees defended it. Paul sided with the Pharisees here. Having seen the risen Christ confirmed the resurrection of the dead. Paul's skillful maneuver worked. An uproar ensued; some sided with Paul, some lined up against him.

Fearing that Paul would be torn to pieces by the mob, Lysias ordered his troops to rescue Paul and take him to their barracks. The following night Our Lord stood by him and said: "Take courage...you will bear witness to my cause in Rome."

How much Paul needed this! On two other occasions, at Corinth (Acts 18:9-10) and during his shipwreck (Act 27:23-24), Our Lord came to Paul to sustain him. The Lord is ever at our side, even when we do not suspect it. He knows, He sees! Paul wondered if he had done right in Jerusalem. Jesus said he had. And now He wanted him to go to Rome to do the same thing. The first step on this journey began with Paul's being transferred to Caesarea.

Acts 23:12 - 25:27

Transfer to Caesarea [12] When day came, the Jews made a plot and bound themselves by oath not to eat or to drink until they had killed Paul [13] There were more than forty who formed this conspiracy. [14] They went to the chief priests and elders and said, "We have bound ourselves by a solemn oath to taste nothing until we have killed Paul. [15] You, together with the Sanhedrin, must now make an official request to the commander to have him bring him down to you, as though you meant to investigate his case more thoroughly. We on our part are prepared to kill him before he arrives." [16] The son of Paul's sister, however, heard about the ambush; so he went and entered the compound and reported it to Paul. [17] Paul then called one of the centurions and requested, "Take this young man to the commander; he has something to report to him." [18] So he took him and brought him to the commander and explained, "The prisoner Paul called me and asked *that I bring this young man* to you; he has something to say to you." [19] The commander took him by the hand, drew him aside, and asked him privately, "What is it you have to report to me?" [20] He replied, "The Jews have conspired to ask you to bring Paul down to the Sanhedrin tomorrow, as though they meant to inquire about him more thoroughly, [21] but do not believe them. More than forty of them are lying in wait for him; they have bound themselves by oath not to eat or drink until they have killed him. They are now ready and only wait for your consent." [22] As the commander dismissed the young man he directed him, "Tell no one that you gave me this information."

[23] Then he summoned two of the centurions and said, "Get two hundred soldiers ready to go to Caesarea by nine o'clock tonight, along with seventy horsemen and two hundred auxiliaries. [24] Provide mounts for Paul to ride and give him safe conduct to Felix the governor." [25] Then he wrote a letter with this content: [26] "Claudius Lysias to his excellency the governor Felix, greetings. [27] This man, seized by the Jews and about to be murdered by them, I rescued after in-

tervening with my troops when I learned that he was a Roman citizen. [28] I wanted to learn the reason for their accusations against him so I brought him down to their Sanhedrin. [29] I discovered that he was accused in matters of controversial questions of their law and not of any charge deserving death or imprisonment. [30] Since it was brought to my attention that there will be a plot against the man, I am sending him to you at once, and have also notified his accusers to state [their case] against him before you."

[31] So the soldiers, according to their orders, took Paul and escorted him by night to Antipatris. [32] The next day they returned to the compound, leaving the horsemen to complete the journey with him. [33] When they arrived in Caesarea they delivered the letter to the governor and presented Paul to him. [34] When he had read it and asked to what province he belonged, and learned that he was from Cilicia, [35] he said, "I shall hear your case when your accusers arrive." Then he ordered that he be held in custody in Herod's praetorium.

24 Trials before Felix [1] Five days later the high priest Ananias came down with some elders and an advocate, a certain Tertullus, and they presented formal charges against Paul to the governor. [2] When he was called, Tertullus began to accuse him, saying, "Since we have attained much peace through you and reforms have been accomplished in this nation through your provident care, [3] we acknowledge this in every way and everywhere, most excellent Felix, with all gratitude. [4] But in order not to detain you further, I ask you to give us a brief hearing with your customary graciousness. [5] We found this man to be a pest; he creates dissension among Jews all over the world and is a ringleader of the sect of the Nazoreans. [6] He even tried to desecrate our temple, but we arrested him. [7] [8] If you examine him you will be able to learn from him for yourself about everything of which we are accusing him." [9] The Jews also joined in the attack and asserted that these things were so.

¹⁰ Then the governor motioned to him to speak and Paul replied, "I know that you have been a judge over this nation for many years and so I am pleased to make my defense before you. ¹¹ As you can verify, not more than 12 days have passed since I went up to Jerusalem to worship. ¹² Neither in the temple, nor in the synagogues, nor anywhere in the city did they find me arguing with anyone or instigating a riot among the people. ¹³ Nor can they prove to you the accusations they are now making against me. ¹⁴ But this I do admit to you, that according to the Way, which they call a sect, I worship the God of our ancestors and I believe everything that is in accordance with the law and written in the prophets. ¹⁵ I have the same hope in God as they themselves have that there will be a resurrection of the righteous and the unrighteous. ¹⁶ Because of this, I always strive to keep my conscience clear before God and man. ¹⁷ After many years, I came to bring alms for my nation and offerings. ¹⁸ While I was so engaged, they found me, after my purification, in the temple without a crowd or disturbance. ¹⁹ But some Jews from the province of Asia, who should be here before you to make whatever accusation they might have against me— ²⁰ or let these men themselves state what crime they discovered when I stood before the Sanhedrin, ²¹ unless it was my one outcry as I stood among them, that 'I am on trial before you today for the *resurrection of the dead.*'"

²² Then Felix, who was accurately informed about the Way, postponed the trial, saying, "When Lysias the commander comes down, I shall decide your case." ²³ He gave orders to the centurion that he should be kept in custody but have some liberty, and that he should not prevent any of his friends from caring for his needs.

Captivity in Caesarea ²⁴ several days later Felix came with his wife Drusilla, who was Jewish. He had Paul summoned and listened to him speak about faith in Christ Jesus. ²⁵ But as he spoke about righteousness and self-restraint and the coming judgment, Felix became frightened and said, "You may go for now; when I find an opportunity I shall summon you agian." ²⁶ At the same time he hoped that a bribe would be offered him by Paul, and so he sent for him very often and conversed with him.

[27] Two years passed and Felix was succeeded by Porcius Festus. Wishing to ingratiate himself with the Jews, Felix left Paul in prison.

25 Appeal to Caesar [1] Three days after his arrival in the province, Festus went up from Caesarea to Jerusalem [2] where the chief priests and Jewish leaders presented him their formal charges against Paul. They asked him [3] as a favor to have him sent to Jerusalem, for they were plotting to kill him along the way. [4] Festus replied that Paul awas being held in custody in Caesarea and that he himself would be returning there shortly. [5] He said, "Let your authorities come down with me, and if this man has done something improper, let them accuse him."

[6] After spending no more than eight or ten days with them, he went down to Caesarea, and on the following day took his seat on the tribunal and ordered that Paul be brought in. [7] When he appeared, the Jews who had come down from Jerusalem surrounded him and brought many serious charges against him, which they were unable to prove. [8] In defending himself Paul said, "I have committed no crime either against the Jewish law or against the temple or against Caesar." [9] Then Festus, wishing to ingratiate himself with the Jews, said to Paul in reply, "Are you willing to go to Jerusalem and there stand trial before me on these charges?" [10] Paul answered, "I am standing before the tribunal of Caesar, this is where I should be tried. I have committed no crime against the Jews, as you very well know. [11] If I have committed a crime or done anything deserving death, I do not seek to escape the death penalty; but if there is no substance to the charges they are bringing against me, then no one has the right to hand me over to them. I appeal to Caesar." [12] Then Festus, after conferring with his council, replied, "You have appealed to Caesar. To Caesar you will go."

Paul before King Agrippa [13] When a few days had passed, King Agrippa and Bernice arrived in Caesarea on a visit to Festus. [14] Since they spent several days there, Festus referred Paul's case to the king, saying, "There is a man here left in custody by Felix. [15] When I was in Jerusalem the chief priests and the elders of the Jews brought charges against him and demanded his condemnation. [16] I answered them that it was not Roman practice to hand over an accused person before he has faced his accusers and had the opportunity to defend himself against their charge. [17] So when [they] came together here, I made no delay; the next day I took my seat on the tribunal and ordered the man to be brought in. [18] His accusers stood around him, but did not charge him with any of the crimes I suspected. [19] Instead they had some issues with him about their own religion and about a certain Jesus who had died but who Paul claimed was alive. [20] Since I was at a loss how to investigate this controversy, I asked if he were willing to go to Jerusalem and there stand trial on these charges. [21] And when Paul appealed that he be held in custody for the Emperor's decision, I ordered him held until I could send him to Caesar." [22] Agrippa said to Festus, "I too should like to hear this man." he replied, "Tomorrow you will hear him."

[23] The next day Agrippa and Bernice came with great ceremony and entered the audience hall in the company of cohort commanders and the prominent men of the city and, by command of Festus, Paul was brought in. [24] And Festus said, "King Agrippa and all you here present with us, look at this man about whom the whole Jewish populace petitioned me here and in Jerusalem, clamoring that he should live no longer. [25] I found, however, that he had done nothing deserving death, and so when he appealed to the Emperor, I decided to send him. [26] but I have nothing definite to write about him to our sovereign; therefore I have brought him before all of you, and particularly before you, King Agrippa, so that I may have something to write as a result of this investigation. [27] For it seems senseless to me to send a prisoner without indicating the charges against him."

Acts 26:1-27:44

26 King Agrippa Hears Paul ¹ Then Agrippa said to Paul, "You may now speak on your own behalf." So Paul stretched out his hand and began his defense. ² "I count myself fortunate, King Agrippa, that I am to defend myself before you today against all the charges made against me by the Jews, ³ especially since you are an expert in all the Jewish customs and controversies. And therefore I beg you to listen patiently. ⁴ My manner of living from my youth, a life spent from the beginning among my people and in Jerusalem, all [the] Jews know. ⁵ They have known about me from the start, if they are willing to testify, that I have lived my life as a Pharisee, the strictest party of our religion. ⁶ But now I am standing trial because of my hope in the promise made by God to our ancestors. ⁷ Our twelve tribes hope to attain to that promise as they fervently worship God day and night; on account of this hope I am accused by Jews, O king. ⁸ Why is it thought unbelievable among you that God raises the dead? ⁹ I myself once thought that I had to do many things against the name of Jesus the Nazorean, ¹⁰ and I did so in Jerusalem. I imprisoned many of the holy ones with the authorization I received from the chief priests, ¹¹ Many times, in synagogue after synagogue, I punished them in an attempt to force them to blaspheme; I was so enraged against them that I pursued them even to foreign cities.

¹² On one such occasion I was traveling to Damascus with the authorization and commission of the chief priests. ¹³ At midday, along the way, O king, I saw a light from the sky, brighter than the sun, shining around me and my traveling companions. ¹⁴ We all fell to the ground and I heard a voice saying to me in Hebrew, *'Saul, Saul, why are you persecuting me? It is hard for you to kick against the goad.'* ¹⁵ And I said, *'Who are you, sir?'* And the Lord replied, *'I am Jesus whom you are persecuting.* ¹⁶ Get up now, and stand on your feet. I have appeared to you for this purpose, to appoint you as a servant and witness of what you have seen [of me] and what you will be shown. ¹⁷ I shall deliver you

from these people and from the Gentiles to whom I send you, [18] to open their eyes that they may turn from darkness to light and from the power of Satan to God, so that they may obtain forgiveness of sins and in inheritance among those who have been consecrated by faith in me.'

[19] "And so, King Agrippa, I was not disobedient to the heavenly vision. [20] On the contrary, first to those in Damascus and in Jerusalem and throughout the whole country of Judea, and then to the Gentiles, I preached the need to repent and turn to God, and to do works giving evidence of repentance. [21] That is why the Jews seized me [when I was] in the temple and tried to kill me. [22] But I have enjoyed God's help to this very day, and so I stand here testifying to small and great alike, saying nothing different from what the prophets and Moses foretold. [23] that the Messiah must suffer and that, as the first to rise from the dead, he would proclaim light both to our people and to the Gentiles."

Reactions to Paul's Speech [24] While Paul was so speaking in his defense, Festus, said in a loud voice, "You are mad, Paul; much learning is driving you mad." [25] But Paul replied, "I am not mad, most excellent Festus; I am speaking words of truth and reason. [26] The king knows about these matters and to him I speak boldly, for I cannot believe that [any] of this has escaped his notice; this was not done in a corner. [27] King Agrippa, do you believe the prophets? I know you believe." [28] Then Agrippa said to Paul, "You will soon persuade me to play the Christian." [29] Paul replied, "I would pray to God that sooner or later not only you but all who listen to me today might become as I am except for these chains."

[30] The king rose, and with him the governor and Bernice and the others who sat with them. [31] And after they had withdrawn they said to one another, "This man is doing nothing [at all] that deserves death or imprisonment." [32] And Agrippa said to Festus, "This man could have been set free if he had not appealed to Caesar."

27 Departure for Rome [1] When it was decided that we should sail to Italy, *they handed Paul and some other* prisoners over to a centurion named Julius of the Cohort Augusta. [2] We went on board a ship from Adramyttium bound for ports in the province of Asia and set sail. Aristarchus, a Macedonian from Thessalonica, was with us. [3] On the following day we put in at Sidon where Julius was kind enough to allow Paul to visit his friends who took care of him. [4] From there we put out to sea and sailed around the sheltered side of Cyprus because of the headwinds, [5] and crossing the open sea off the coast of Cilicia and Pamphylia we came to Myra in Lycia.

Storm and Shipwreck [6] There the centurion found an Alexandrian ship that was sailing to Italy and put us on board. [7] For many days we made little headway, arriving at Cnidus only with difficulty, and because the wind would not permit us to continue our course sailed for the sheltered side of Crete off Salmone. [8] We sailed past it with difficulty and reached a place called Fair Havens, near which was the city of Lasea.

[9] Much time had now passed and sailing had become hazardous because the time of the fast had already gone by, so Paul warned them, [10] "Men, I can see that this voyage will result in severe damage and heavy loss not only to the cargo and the ship, but also to our lives." [11] The centurion, however, paid more attention to the pilot and to the owner of the ship than to what Paul said. [12] Since the harbor was unfavorable situated for spending the winter, the majority planned to put out to sea from there in the hope of reaching Phoenix, a port in Crete facing west-northwest, there to spend the winter.

[13] A south wind blew gently, and thinking they had attained their objective, they weighed anchor and sailed along close to the coast of Crete. [14] Before long an offshore wind of hurricane force called a "Northeaster" struck. [15] Since the ship was caught up in it and could not head into the wind we gave way and let ourselves be driven. [16] We passed along the sheltered side of an island named Cauda and managed only with difficulty to get the dinghy under control.

[17] They hoisted it aboard, then used cables to undergird the ship. Because of their fear that they would run aground on the shoal of Syrtis, they lowered the drift anchor and were carried along in this way. [18] We were being pounded by the storm so violently that the next day they jettisoned some cargo, [19] and on the third day with their own hands they threw even the ship's tackle overboard. [20] Neither the sun nor the stars were visible for many days, and no small storm raged. Finally, all hope of our surviving was taken away.

[21] When many would no longer eat, Paul stood among them and said, "Men, you should have taken my advice and not have set sail from Crete and you would have avoided this disastrous loss. [22] I urge you now to keep up your courage; not one of you will be lost, only the ship. [23] For last night an angel of the God to whom [I] belong and whom I serve stood by me [24] and said, 'Do not be afraid, Paul. You are destined to stand before Caesar: and behold, for your sake, God has granted safety to all who are sailing with you,' [25] Therefore, keep up your courage, men; I trust in God that it will turn out as I have been told. [26] We are destined to run aground on some island."

[27] On the fourteenth night, as we were still being driven about on the Adriatic Sea, toward midnight the sailors began to suspect that they were nearing land. [28] They took sounding and found twenty fathoms; a little farther on, they again took soundings and found fifteen fathoms. [29] Fearing that we would run aground on a rocky coast, they dropped four anchors from the stern and prayed for day to come. [30] The sailors then tried to abandon ship; they lowered the dinghy to the sea on the pretext of going to lay out anchors from the bow. [31] But Paul said to the centurion and the soldier." "Unless these men stay with the ship, you cannot be saved." [32] So the soldiers cut the ropes of the dinghy and set it adrift.

[33] Until the day began to dawn, Paul kept urging all to take some food. He said, "Today is the fourteenth day that you have been waiting, going hungry and eating nothing. [34] I urge you, therefore, to take some food; it will help you survive. Not a hair of the head of anyone of you will be

lost." [35] When he said this, he took bread, gave thanks to God in front of them all, broke it, and began to eat. [36] They were all encouraged, and took some food themselves. [37] In all, there were two hundred seventy-six of us on the ship. [38] After they had eaten enough, they lightened the ship by throwing the wheat into the sea.

[39] When day came they did not recognize the land, but made out a bay with a beach. They planned to run the ship ashore on it, if they could. [40] So they cast off the anchors and abandoned them to the sea, and at the same time they unfastened the lines of the rudders, and hoisting the foresail into the wind, they made for the beach. [41] But they struck a sandbar and ran the ship aground. The bow was wedged in and could not be moved, but the stern began to break up under the pounding [of the waves]. [42] The soldiers planned to kill the prisoners so that none might swim away and escape. [43] but the centurion wanted to save Paul and so kept them from carrying out their plan. He ordered those who could swim to jump overboard first and get to the shore, [44] and then the rest , some on planks, others on debris from the ship. In this way, all reached shore safely.

Acts 28:1-31

28 Winter in Malta [1] Once we had reached safety we learned that the island was called Malta. [2] The Natives showed us extraordinary hospitality; they lit a fire and welcomed all of us because it had begun to rain and was cold. [3] Paul had gathered a bundle of brushwood and was putting it on the fire when a viper, escaping from the heat, fastened on his hand.. [4] When the natives saw the snake hanging from his hand, they said to one another, " This man must certainly be a murderer though he escaped the sea, . Justice has not let him remain alive." [5] But he shook the snake off into the fire and suffered no harm. [6] They were expecting him to swell up or suddenly to fall down dead but, after waiting a long time and seeing nothing unusual happen to him, they changed their minds and began to say that he was a god. [7] In the vicinity of that place were lands belonging to a man named Publius, the chief of the island. He welcomed us and received us cordially as his guests for three days. [8] It so happened that the father of Publius was sick with a fever and dysentery. Paul visited him and, after praying, laid his hands on him and healed him. [9] After this had taken place, the rest of the sick on the island came to Paul and were cured. [10] They paid us great honor and when we eventually set sail they brought us the provisions we needed.

Arrival in Rome [11] Three months later we set sail on a ship that had wintered at the island. It was an Alexandrian ship with the Dioscuri as its figurehead. [12] We put in at Syracuse and stayed there three days, [13] and from there we sailed round the coast and arrived at Rhegium. After a day, a south wind came up and in two days we reached Putcoli. [14] There we found some brothers and were urged to stay with them for seven days. And thus we came to Rome. [15] The brothers from there heard about us and came as far as the Forum of Appius and Three Taverns to meet us. On seeing them, Paul gave thanks to God and took courage. [16] When he entered Rome, Paul was allowed to live by himself, with the soldier who was guarding him.

Testimony to Jews in Rome [17] Three days later he called together the leaders of the Jews. When they had gathered he said to them, "My brothers, although I had done nothing against our people or our ancestral customs, I was handed over to the Romans as a prisoner from Jerusalem. [18] After trying my case the Romans wanted to release me, because they found nothing against me deserving the death penalty. [19] But when the Jews objected, I was obliged to appeal to Caesar, even though I had no accusation to make against my own nation. [20] This is the reason, then, I have requested to see you and to speak with you, for it is on account of the hope of Israel that I wear these chains." [21] They answered him, "We have received no letters from Judea about you, nor has any of the brothers arrived with a damaging report or rumor about you. [22] But we should like to hear you present your views, for we know that this sect is denounced everywhere."

²³ So they arranged the day with him and came to his lodgings in great numbers. From early morning until evening he expounded his position to them, bearing witness to the kingdom of God and trying to convince them about Jesus from the law of Moses and the prophets. ²⁴ Some were convinced by what he had said, while others did not believe. ²⁵ Without *reaching any agreement* among themselves they began to leave; then Paul made one final statement, "Well did the Holy Spirit speak to your ancestors through the prophet Isaiah, saying:

²⁶ 'Go to this people and say:
You shall indeed hear but not understand.
You shall indeed look but never see.
²⁷ Gross is the heart of this people;
they will not hear with their ears;
they have closed their eyes,
so they may not see with their eyes
and hear with their ears
and understand with their heart and be converted,
and I heal them.'

²⁸ Let it be known to you that this salvation of God has been sent to the Gentiles; they will listen." [29]

³⁰ He remained for two full years in his lodgings. He received all who came to him, ³¹ and with complete assurance and without hindrance he proclaimed the kingdom of God and taught about the Lord Jesus Christ.

CHAPTER 15

The Road to Rome

Transfer to Caesarea (23:12-35). Foiled by Paul's defense, the Jews plotted to kill Paul. At least forty young men, studying at the rabbinical schools and trying to ingratiate themselves with the Sanhedrin, bound themselves neither to eat nor to drink until they had killed him. Their plot had the approval of the Sanhedrin. How low the government of the nation had fallen! A heathen government, like Rome's made life more secure and justice more sure than that of the professed people of God. What a contrast, too, was Claudius Lysias to the High Priest! Claudius knew his duty, was prompt in action, loyal to the Empire, courteous to Paul.

This conspiracy, however, was thwarted by Paul's nephew. his sister's son. Somehow or other, Paul's nephew got wind of the conspiracy. He went to Paul and Paul sent him to Lysias. The commander took the lad aside to speak with him privately. Eager to redeem his previous error of maltreating a Roman citizen, Claudius arranged for Paul's removal from Jerusalem.

He ordered 200 infantry, 70 cavalry and 200 spearmen to conduct Paul from the city at night. How grave must have been the threat to Paul's life that required 400 men to insure his safety. The soldiers escorted Paul to Antipatris, 40 miles from Jerusalem and halfway to Caesarea; from there, the entire contingent returned to Jerusalem with the exception of the cavalry which took Paul to Caesarea.

The Roman Governor at Caesarea was Marcus Antonius Felix, Procurator of Judea from 52 to 60 A.D. Felix, according to the Roman historian Tacitus, indulged in every kind of barbarity and lust;

he exercised the power of a king in the spirit of a slave. He was known for his cruelty toward and oppression of his Jewish subjects.

Lysias in his letter to Felix stated that Paul was innocent of anything deserving punishment. Being a Roman citizen, he deserved the protection of the Procurator against those plotting to take his life. Lysias was passing the buck; but it brought Paul to Caesarea.

Trial before Felix (24:1-23). Paul's trial before Felix took place five days after his arrival in Caesarea. The High Priest Ananias came with certain elders and the lawyer Tertullus before Felix to make formal charges against Paul. Tertullus was probably a Roman lawyer, for very likely, the Jews were ignorant of Roman procedure.

In the first century trials were not run as they are today. Lawyers were really rhetoricians. They were trained, not in the technicalities of law, but in the art of persuasion, of how to persuade judges. Both Paul and Tertullus used this technique.

Tertullus began with profuse flattery of Felix. Then he indicted Paul, "This man," he charged, " is a pest, a creator of dissension, a ringleader of the Nazoreans, a desecrator of the Temple. Ask him for yourself and see that this is so." The Jews joined in the attack and asserted that these things were so.

Then the governor motioned to Paul to speak. Unlike Tertullus, Paul used no flattering introduction to Felix, but only respect. He recognized that Felix was authorized judge of the nation. Then he went on to say that he had been in Jerusalem only twelve days— surely too short a time to start a sedition.

Paul admitted that the Way of Christianity, which they had labeled a sect, formed a continuity with Judaism. For he still worshipped the same God the other Jews did and believed in the resurrection of the dead. He explained that he had come to Jerusalem to bring alms to the Church there. Mention of alms no doubt sowed the idea of a possible bribe in Felix's mind. So He postponed the trial on the pretext of awaiting Lysias' arrival. Lysias had already given his report in his letter. But Felix was corrupt, cruel and venal. He hoped for a bribe. So he ordered that Paul be held in loose custody and his friends be allowed to care for his needs.

Captivity in Caesarea (24:24-27). Several days later, Felix came with his wife Drusilla, who was Jewish. He had Paul summoned and listened to him speak about faith in Jesus Christ. Paul spoke to Felix about righteousness (about being a just judge), about self-restraint (being moral and chaste) and about the coming judgment (his having to give an account for his actions). Felix became frightened. So he dismissed Paul. Like Herod, he had reason to fear; for, through the help of Simon Magus, he had taken Drusilla, a Jew and daughter of Herod Agrippa I, from her husband Azizus of Emesa to become his third wife. Neither of them were models of virtue.

The jailer at Philippi became frightened at Paul's word, but he yielded to the gospel. Felix feared, but he did not yield. He should have released Paul; but no, he hoped for a bribe and thus conversed with him often. The jailer at Philippi wanted to be saved; Felix wanted to give Paul an opportunity to offer him a bribe.

Intellectually curiosity is never enough to embrace Christianity; a moral disposition is needed, for Christianity is not a philosophical system, but a complete surrender to a person, to Christ. Immorality and greed closed the mind of Felix to the gospel. Even today the opposition to the Church is not intellectual, but moral; the objection is not so much to the dogma of three Persons in one God, but to the Christian morality that divorce, contraception, abortion are wrong.

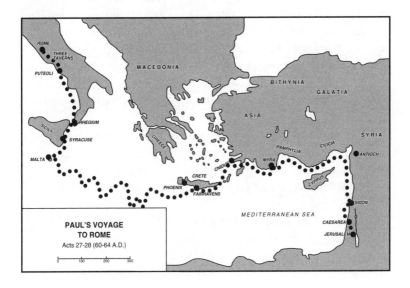

PAUL'S VOYAGE TO ROME
Acts 27-28 (60-64 A.D.)

In 60 A.D., Felix was removed from office because of his slaughter of some Jews and his plundering them during an insurrection. He probably went to Rome with Drusilla, and Simon Magus tagged along as a domestic chaplain. A deputation of Jews also followed him to Rome, to prosecute him before the emperor Nero. They succeeded in getting back much of the plunder Felix had taken. Palla, Felix's brother, and a friend of Nero, was able to prevent further punishment. Felix disappears out of history. But Drusilla reappeared nineteen years later, at the hot spots around the Bay of Naples, with her grown-up boy, Agrippa. Both died in Pompeii when the city was destroyed by Vesuvius (79 A.D.) Porcius Festus succeeded Felix as Procurator of Judea (60-62 A.D.)

Appeal to Caesar (25:1-12). After three days, Festus went up to Jerusalem. The chief priests and Jewish leaders presented formal charges against Paul. You would think that after two years, they would have forgotten Paul. Had his offense been personal, they might have. But they rightly saw Paul as overturning Judaism. Hence their undying hatred.

They asked Festus to bring Paul to trial in Jerusalem, intending to murder him. Festus sensed that something was wrong, so he invited them to come to Caesarea. After eight or ten days in Jerusalem, Festus returned to Caesarea. The very next day, he called Paul to trial. Two years of imprisonment had neither broken Paul's courage nor weakened his mind. He pointed out that the Jews had no grounds to prove their charges. Festus should have released Paul then and there. However, popularity was dearer to him than justice. To ingratiate himself with the Jews, Festus proposed a trial in Jerusalem.

Paul had had it! So he appealed to Caesar, which was his right as a Roman citizen. Festus, after conferring with his council, replied, "You have appealed to Caesar. To Caesar you will go." God had told Paul he would go to Rome; the Jews had plotted to kill him. But God won out—Paul was to go to Rome.

Paul before King Agrippa (25:13-27). Festus found himself in an embarrassing situation: he was sending a prisoner to Caesar against whom he had no charge. King Agrippa II and his sister Bernice had come to Festus to pay a courtesy call. Festus was delighted, for he hoped Agrippa could help uncover some charge in

Paul's case. Agrippa was half-Jew; and the accusation was a religious, not a political one: "about a certain Jesus who had died but whom Paul claimed was alive."

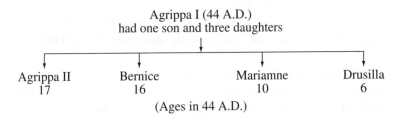

Agrippa I (44 A.D.)
had one son and three daughters

| Agrippa II | Bernice | Mariamne | Drusilla |
| 17 | 16 | 10 | 6 |

(Ages in 44 A.D.)

At the time of his visit to Festus, Agrippa II was about 33. He lived to be 73, and died in the reign of Trajan. Bernice's history read like that of the Borgias. She married her uncle, and he died. Then she married the king of Cilicia and left him. Rumor had it that she was having an incestuous relationship with her brother, Agrippa II. Later she became the mistress of the Emperor Titus; but public opinion forced him to dismiss her, which he unwillingly did, according to Suetonius.

King Agrippa Hears Paul (26:1-23). Agrippa was happy to hear Paul, but for the wrong reason: curiosity. So he and Bernice came in sumptuous splendor for another diversion.

Agrippa gave Paul permission to speak, to state his case. Paul began by trying to win the goodwill of Agrippa by acknowledging him as an expert in Jewish customs and controversies. Then he resorted to his favorite argument: "I was a Pharisee, an ardent one, yea a feared persecutor of the Way. Then all of a sudden I changed. You know why? I had a vision of the glorified Christ on the road to Damascus. It happened at midday."

Generally, no one traveled during the midday heat. Paul did; he must have been in a desperate hurry. Undoubtedly, his violent activity against the Church was an effort to silence his conscience, which had been pricking him ever since the martyrdom of St. Stephen. Jesus alluded to this inner conflict, when He said, "Saul, Saul, why are you persecuting me? It is hard for you to kick against the goad."

How tender Jesus was, He spoke to Saul by name. Knows him. Then He identified Himself with His Church; what Saul was doing to her, he was really doing to Christ. Jesus' words were a kind of lament: "What have I done to merit your persecution? Your hatred and not your Love? You are not hurting me by your persecution, but yourself, as a young ox does by kicking against the goad. Why are you acting like an animal?"

Paul then went on to tell Agrippa of his mission: to turn all people from darkness to light, from the dominion of Satan to God, and from sin to the forgiveness of sin.

As regards Christ, he told Agrippa, I have seen Him risen. As regards to Gentiles, I have been commissioned by God to preach to them. I could not disobey God. The Jews call me a heretic; but they, not I, are the heretics, for Moses and the prophets foretold that the Messiah would suffer, die, and rise. I simply hold the essential doctrines of Judaism: the hope of a Messiah. Where I differ from the Jews is in this: I believe the Messiah is Christ and that salvation is for both the Jews and the Gentiles."

Reactions to Paul's Speech (26:24-32). As Paul went on with great fervor, Festus rudely interrupted him. In a loud voice he said, "You are mad, Paul." To speak of visions, of a risen Christ, of sin, repentance, forgiveness, to become a social outcast among the Greeks and the Jews, as Paul had done, was madness to Festus. However, to soften his harsh accusation, Festus added, "Your great learning is driving you mad." Festus no doubt knew of Paul's having studied under Gamaliel. Also Paul might have shown great anxiety to have books (2 Tm. 4:3). You can be sure that during his two years of imprisonment, Paul had been studying and his cell must have been filled with scrolls.

Paul obliquely rebukes Festus by turning to Agrippa and saying in effect, "It's not surprising to hear you think like that, because you are not a Jew. But the king knows what I am talking about, for all these things did not happen in a dark corner." Agrippa was moved and said to Paul, "You will soon persuade me to play the Christian."

What blocked Agrippa from becoming a Christian? Many things.

First, there was his worldliness: love of office and distinction, love of a particular sin (incest with Bernice). Worldly people are those who prefer pleasure to right; the visible to the invisible; the passing to the eternal; and the material to the spiritual. So here, to the worldly and voluptuous Agrippa, Paul's preaching meant nothing.

Then there was the fear of shame. Festus had called Paul mad; should Agrippa follow him, Festus might have said, "Ah, two madmen."

What a critical moment in Agrippa's life! "You will soon persuade me." As Pilate, not Jesus, was being judged when Jesus stood before him; so here, Agrippa, not Paul was being judged. His fate was being determined. Forty years later, Agrippa died as he had lived.

Paul saw he was getting nowhere, so he wound up his defense with a prayer. The upshot of all this was that Paul again was declared innocent. But since he had appealed to Caesar, he had to go to Rome.

Departure for Rome (27:1-5). The voyage to Rome started in the late summer of 60 A.D. With Paul was Luke and a Thessalonian, Aristarchus. Two companions or slaves were permitted a Roman citizen when traveling as a prisoner. The fact that Paul was entrusted to the Cohort Augusta, under a centurion named Julius, was a reflection on his prominence and prestige.

At Caesarea Paul, with his companions and other prisoners boarded ship. The next day they stopped at Sidon, where Julius was kind enough to let Paul visit the church there. Then they set sail around the sheltered side of Cyprus, because of the strong headwinds. Crossing the open sea along the coasts of Cilicia and Pamphylia, they came to Myra.

Storm and Shipwreck (27:6-44). At Myra, Julius found an Alexandrian vessel headed for Italy. He transferred his prisoners to this ship. It made Cnidus with difficulty. Then sailed around the sheltered side of Crete and along the coast to Fair Havens.

It was late September. In September navigation was dangerous. In fact, it ceased from November to March. Paul warned the crew to winter at Fair Havens. But they did not listen to him. Instead they decided to sail to Phoenix, forty miles farther, and winter there because of the better harbor.

They weighed anchor and sailed hugging the coast of Crete. Then all of a sudden a wind of hurricane force, called a "Northeaster," blew. There was nothing to do but to let the ship be driven by the wind. They managed with difficulty to hoist on board the dinghy, used for unloading cargo. Next, they girded the hull with cables to reinforce it. Then because of fear of being driven on the quicksand of Syrtis, off the shores of Tripoli, they lowered the drift anchor.

The storm did not abate, so the next day, they jettisoned some of the cargo; on the third day, some of the ship's gear. For many days neither sun nor stars were visible to help them navigate. The storm raged until all hope of surviving was given up. To their gloom was added exhaustion from their labors and from lack of nutrition, because many would no longer eat.

One person kept his head in all this: the prisoner Paul. He spoke up and said in effect, "you wouldn't listen to me about no sailing from Fair Havens. Maybe you will listen to me now. An angel of God promised that there would be the loss of the ship, but not of life. All will survive, so keep up your courage!"

Paul's effect on the ship contrast to Jonah's. Jonah brought distress on the ship because of his sinfulness. Paul on the contrary was the salvation of his ship. Both were prophets. Paul prophesied that he would stand trial in Rome and his shipmates would be saved.

On the fourteenth night, the sailors began to suspect they were approaching land. They took soundings: 20 fathoms (120 feet), the 15 fathoms. Fearing they would run aground they dropped four anchors from the stern and prayed for day to come. The sailors were going to abandon ship; but Paul prevented this.

At daybreak, Paul urged all to take some food. He himself took bread, gave thanks, broke it and began to eat (probably celebrated the Eucharist). This encouraged the rest to follow suit. There were 276 persons aboard. After having eaten, they lightened the ship by throwing the wheat cargo into the sea.

When day came, they saw land. Trying to steer the ship into a bay, they hit a sandbar. The pounding of the waves began to break up the ship. The soldiers planned to kill the prisoners lest they escape. However, Julius forbade this in order to save the life of Paul. As Paul had prophesied, the ship was lost, but all 276 made it safely to shore.

Just a few reflections here.

1. Often the so-called experts are prone to reject the advice of religious persons. Paul warned them not to set sail from Fair Havens. The "experts" ignored his warning.

2. The value of our possessions is relative. In times of severe trials, they often become burdens, like baggage to an army (*impedmenta*) Still we reluctantly part with them. Yet in the end, to save their lives, the sailors on Paul's ship jettisoned everything. Detachment from our earthly possessions is also necessary if we are to arrive at the port of heaven.

3. When storms come, Christians should speak out, as did Paul to impart good courage to others.

4. The good suffer with the bad. Paul, Luke and Aristarchus with criminals. Yet how differently: Paul and his companions were of good cheer; the others were full of fear.

5. A ship in water is good; but water in a ship is bad. So it is all right for a Christian to be in the world; but not all right for the world to be in a Christian.

6. A farmer had inscribed on his weathervane the words: "God is love."

   Someone asked him: "Does God's love change with the winds?"

   "No," answered the farmer, "It means that God is love no matter which way the winds blow."

7. Paul had foretold that no one on board would be lost. The sailors disbelieved; they planned to escape. Paul told the centurion that if the sailors fled, they could not be saved. Their skill was needed to bring the ship close to shore. So prayer requires human efforts, cooperation. Pray as if all depended on God; yet work as if all depended on self.

8. In the new Testament nothing is more remarkable that the favorable impression of Roman officers given by its writers. Can it be that the military career fosters many attractive virtues? Or does Scripture remind us that one can become virtuous even in the adverse circumstances of military life?

There was the centurion at Capernaum, whose words we say at each Mass: "O Lord, I am not worthy..." (Mk. 8:10:Lk.7:(9); the centurion at the cross, St. Longinus (Mk. 15:39: Lk. 34:47); the centurion Cornelius, the first Gentile to be received officially into the Church (Act 10:1; 11:18). In Paul's life, centurions played a major part; to mention only two: Lysias, Julius.

How wrong it is for extreme pacifists to condemn the military. At least twice, the military saved Paul's life. They respected Paul, and Paul esteemed them.

Winter in Malta (28:1-10). Once the shipwrecked people reached safety, they learned that the island on which they had landed was called Malta, south of Sicily. The inhabitants spoke a Phoenician dialect, similar to Aramaic. They were really kind and extended great hospitality to the survivors. They lit a fire to warm them from a chilling rain.

As always, Paul was there to help; he had gathered a bundle of brushwood and was about to put it in the fire when a viper escaping from the heat fastened on his hand. The natives inferred that Paul must have been a great criminal, saved from the sea, only to die by a viper's fang. Even heathen believed in the retributive justice of God.

How prone everyone is to make rash judgments. It is easy to be sure that other people deserve their punishment and are getting it when calamity strikes. But if trouble touches us, we wonder why God is afflicting us. At least we don't think we are at fault. But if trouble comes to our neighbors, we conclude quickly enough where the trouble lies.

The natives were guilty of rash judgment at first but when Paul did not swell up and die, they went to the other extreme and considered him a god.

In the vicinity was a man named Publius, the chief of the island. He welcomed and entertained Paul and his companions for three days. The father of Publius was sick with fever and dysentery; instead of having Luke the physician look after him, Paul prayed, laid hands on him, and healed him. Religion can be a greater healer than medicine. Paul did not preach here; he simply healed everybody. The people were so grateful that they provisioned them with all they needed for the final leg of their journey.

Arrival in Rome (28:11-16). After three months on the island, when winter had past and spring was approaching, Paul and the others set sail in an Alexandrian ship that had wintered in Malta. The figurehead on its prow was that of the Twins, Castor and Pollux, Jupiter's twin sons and patron of sailors. They sailed north to Syracuse, the chief seaport of Sicily, and stayed there three days. Then they went to Rhegium on the toe of Italy. From there, they sailed to Puteoli, near Naples, the great mercantile seaport of Rome, and spent seven days there.

Word was sent to Rome of Paul's coming. As he traveled up the Appian Way, a delegation from Rome went out to meet him at the Forum Appius, 43 miles south of Rome and at Three Taverns, 33 miles south of Rome. Paul was delighted to meet the brothers here. Three years earlier he had written an Epistle to them. Paul thanked God and took courage. As iron sharpen iron; so friends cheer friends. At Rome Paul was given considerable freedom, even though chained constantly to a soldier guard, 61 A.D.

Testimony to Jew in Rome (28:17-30). Paul did not bring the faith to Rome; he brought a last appeal to the Jews of Rome to receive the faith. One of the great themes of Acts was to explain why the Church founded in Judaism is chiefly Gentile. It was not because of Paul's apostasy, but because the Jews had rejected the gospel.

Paul's imprisonment lasted four years: two in Caesarea and two in Rome. His Roman imprisonment was most fruitful.

His lodging place became as the shrine of an oracle. Every day visitors came in great numbers. From morning till evening, Paul tried to convince them about Jesus from the law of Moses and the prophets. He had some successes, some failures. To those who did not believe, Paul applied the words of the prophet Isaiah: "Gross is the heart of this people...they will not hear, they have closed their eyes..." (6:9-10). This passage appears in all four gospels and in Romans to explain why Israel rejected her Messiah. Paul concluded that what Israel had rejected would be accepted by the Gentiles — "they will listen."

Paul attracted all kinds of people; for instance, a runaway slave, Onesimus, whom he converted and then sent back to his master, Philemon at Colossae, with letters to Philemon to the Colossians and to the Ephesians. He attracted the young like Timothy and Luke, Mark and Aristarchus, Tychicus, and Epaphras. He sent them out to bring him news of the churches and to carry his messages to them. They responded. Thus the Philippians sent Epaphroditus with money to help him. Perhaps this prompted Paul's letter to the Philippians.

For two full years (61-62 A.D.), Paul remained captive and very busy. Acts ends abruptly here. One of the reasons is, because the preaching of the gospel is never to end till the end of the world; and the other reason is, Luke had fulfilled his purpose, which was to tell of how the gospel came to Judea, Samaria and the ends of the earth.[1]

---

[1]   Released in 63 A.D. Paul appears to have departed immediately on his longest missionary journey, to Spain. On July 18, 64 A.D. the burning of Rome ignited the Neronian persecution. Paul returned from Spain and went directly to Greece. He was arrested in 66 A.D. at Troy and taken a prisoner to Rome.

The next year (67 A.D.), both he and Peter were martyred. Paul was beheaded three miles outside of Rome on the Ostian Way near the world famous basilica of St. Paul's Outside the Walls; and Peter was crucified, out of humility, head downward, on Vatican Hill.

[2]   See Appendix 2 : Chronology for Acts.

APPENDIX 1

THE PONTIFICATE OF ST. PETER, 30-67

30-37	head of the Church in Jerusalem
38-39	missionary journeys in Samaria and on the coast of Palestine
40-41	in Antioch
42	imprisonment in Jerusalem, escape, and departure thence
42-29	*first sojourn in Rome*
49	expulsion from Rome by the edict of Claudius against its Jews
49-50	in Jerusalem for the Apostolic Council
50-54	in Antioch, Bithynia, Pontus; and Cappadocia (or some of them)
54-57	*second sojourn in Rome;* Gospel of Mark written under Peter's direction
57-62	in Bithynia, Pontus, and Cappadocia (or some of them); Mark in Alexandria
62-67	*third sojourn* in Rome; canonical Epistles of Peter; Mark with Peter in Rome
67	martyrdom in Rome and burial at the Vatican

From - Warren H. Carroll, *The Founding of Christendom,* Vol 1, p 422

APPENDIX 2

Chronology for Acts

Date	Events	Palestinian Rulers	Roman Emperors
5/19/30	Jesus' Ascension **(Acts 1)**	Herod Antipas 4 BC-39 AD	Tiberius 14-37
5/29/30	Pentecost **(Acts 2)**		
30-50	Growth of Church at Jerusalem **(Acts 3-6)**	Pontius Pilate Procurator 26-36	
37 spring	Stoning of Stephen **(Acts 7)**		
	Conversion of Ethiopian Eunuch **(Acts 8)**		
37 summer	Conversion of Saul **(Acts 9)**		Caligula 37-41
39	Saul's Return to Jerusalem **(Acts 9)**		
40	Conversion of Cornelius **(Acts 10-11)**		
42	Matyrdom of James **(Acts 12)**	Herod Agrippa I King 41-44	Claudius 41-54

Date	Events	Palestinian Rulers	Roman Emperors
45-49	Paul's First Missionary Journey **(Acts 13-14)**		
50	Council of Jerusalem (Acts 15)		
50-53	Paul's Second Missionary Journey (Acts 15-18) *1 and 2 Thessalonians*	M. Antonius Felix Procurator 52-60	
54-58	Paul's Third Missionary Journey (Acts 18-21 *1 and 2 Corinthians, Galatians, Romans*	Herod Agrippa II 53-70	Nero 54-68
58	Paul's Imprisonment at Jerusalem (Acts 21-23)		
58-60	Pauls Imprisonment at Caesarea (Acts 23-26)	Porcius Festus Procurator 60-62	
60-61	Paul's Journey to Rome (Acts 27-28)		
61-63	Paul's Imprisonment at Rome (Acts 28) *Ephesians, Philippians, Colossians, Philemon*		

APPENDIX 3

A Chronology of the New Testament

1. Birth of St. Joseph

In the year 35-25 B.C. sexual passion played a major role in history: Anthony had an adulterous affair with Cleopatra in Egypt and Herod the Great was madly in love with Mariamne, even though he had murdered her grandfather Hyrcanus and her brother Aristobolus.

Herod's sister, Salome, concocted a story about Mariamne being unfaithful, so Herod murdered her too, and went almost mad with grief.

It was probably within the context of these sexual evils that the ever-chaste St. Joseph, head of the Holy Family, was born in Bethlehem of Judea between the years 35-25 B.C.

Joseph and Mary were betrothed about 7 B.C.

Joseph was probably 25 years old at the time; Mary about 14 or 15.

2. Joachim and Anne

The names of the parents of the Blessed Virgin Mary do not appear in the New Testament; but they do appear in one of the most reliable of the Apocrypha, The Protevangelium of James, written not too long after the gospel of St. John; that is, about 130-140 A.D.

In view of the tenacious genealogical memory or ancient and rural peoples, and especially of the Jews, it is highly unlikely that the names of Mary's parents were forgotten or confused at this early date.

3. **Birth of Mary**

Herod the Great began rebuilding the Temple in Jerusalem in January 19 B.C. The construction went on till 64 A.D.

Probably only a year or two before the beginning of the rebuilding of the Temple, the Blessed Virgin Mary was born in the little village of Nazareth about 21 or 20 B.C.

As the Temple of stone and wood and costly ornaments was rising, she whose womb was to temple God incarnate was growing up at the same time.

Herod was rebuilding a marble temple to the God of the Jews; whereas God Himself was building a *dignum habitaculum,* immaculately conceived in the womb of good St. Anne.

4. **The Annunciation**

a. "Hail Mary, full of grace, the Lord is with you" (Lk. 1:28 Douay-Rheims).

"Hail, favored one! The Lord is with you" (Revised New Testament).

The Greek *kecharitomene* means "one endowed with favor or grace *(charis)* in permanent fashion.

Luke was a disciple of St. Paul. And Paul had developed the whole theology of grace. Luke, therefore chose a word that indicates he understood that a far more than ordinary favor was involved here. The Church teaches that Mary was conceived immaculate from the very first instance of her conception.

b. Mary had made a vow of perpetual virginity before the Annunciation.

Often objections are raised against this on two grounds:

First, on a philological ground. Some say that Mary's question to the angel referred to her immediate present condition of being unmarried.

Ans. The present tense of Mary's words in Luke 1:34 in the Greek correspond, not to the Hebrew and Aramaic Perfect tense indicating a condition limited to the past or present, but to the Hebrew and Aramaic Active Participle indicating a permanent condition.

Second, on a historical ground. Some say consecrated virginity was unknown among the Jews of Mary's day. Ans. This is not true. The Essenes at Qumran were celibate. One might just as well reject the Incarnation on the same grounds that it too was uncommon.

5. **The Birth of Jesus**

The one date that is certain is that of the death of Herod the Great. He died 4 B.C.

Jesus was born before Herod died.

At least 40 days, because Joseph and Mary would never have taken Him to the Temple had Herod ordered Him to be killed.

And then a few more days until the visit of the Magi.

In the last weeks of his life, Herod resided in Jericho, seeking relief from the pains of his fatal illness at the hot springs there.

But the wise men visited Herod in Jerusalem, not at Jericho.

These intervals are enough to push the date of Jesus' birth back to at least 5 B.C.

Most likely, Jesus was born around 6.B.C.

We say this for two reasons.

First, because of the astronomical evidence regarding the star of Bethlehem.

Secondly, because of the **census** at Jesus' birth. "This was the first enrollment when Quirinius was governor of Syria" (Lk.2:2). Quirinius was governor of Syria twice: once before 8 B.C. and once after 4 A.D. Saturninus was governor of Syria from 8 to 6 B.C. Now Quirinius could have begun the census in 6 B.C. completed by Quirinius in 3 B.C.

Tertullian says the census was under Saturninus (p 312 fn.49). This could well have been. But Roman governors often were assisted by one second in command for specific purposes, like a census. Under Saturninus, Quirinius was the military commander in the region. He could have been the one executing the census.

Most likely, Jesus was not born before 6 B.C., because St. Luke says, "When Jesus began his ministry he was about 30 years of age" (3:23). Dating Jesus' birth at 6 B.C. makes Him about 33 years old at the beginning of His public ministry in 28 A.D.

6. Death of St. Joseph

Tradition says that St. Joseph died in 15 A.D. Jesus was about 20 years old then. So for more than a decade, Jesus supported His mother by his carpentering.

7. The Beginning of the Public Ministry of Jesus

St. Luke says that the word of God came to John in the desert in the fifteenth year of the reign of Tiberius Caesar (Lk. 3:1).

Augustus died August 19, 14 A.D. and Tiberius succeeded him. In Syria the new year began in October. Since August to October would be considered the first year of Tiberius' reign, the fifteenth year of Tiberius Caesar would be October 27 A.D.

Tiberius had exiled himself to Capri in 26 A.D. and appointed Pontius Pilate governor of Judea 26-36 A.D.

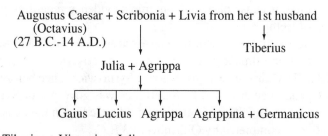

Augustus Caesar + Scribonia + Livia from her 1st husband
(Octavius)
(27 B.C.-14 A.D.)   Tiberius

Julia + Agrippa

Gaius Lucius Agrippa Agrippina + Germanicus

Tiberius + Vipsania + Julia
(14-37 A.D.)

Drusus + Livilla (sister of Germanicus)

8. **The Public Life of Christ**

In the winter of 27 A.D. John the Baptizer baptized Jesus. Shortly after this, perhaps in January or February 28 A.D., Jesus withdrew to Jebel Garantal, the Mount of the Forty Days, overlooking Jericho, to fast and pray for forty days.

After His victory over the temptations of Satan, Jesus came down the mountain and went back to the Jordan where John was still baptizing. When John saw Him, he said, "Behold the Lamb of God"; and two of his disciples, John and Andrew, followed Jesus. Andrew brought his brother Peter to Jesus.

Jesus with these three, headed northward to Galilee. On the way Jesus called Philip. Near Bethel, where Jacob sixteen centuries before had his vision of a ladder going to heaven, Philip got Nathanael (later, Bartholomew) a native of Cana.

At Cana, Jesus joined His mother at the wedding feast there. He changed a 150 gallons of water into wine to teach that He had come to bring joy to the world and to bless marriage.

Then He turned about and headed for Jerusalem to begin His public life at the Passover of March 28 A.D.

9. **The Public Life of Christ, 28 - 30 A.D.**

There were three Passovers in the life of Jesus:
at the beginning of His public life 28 A.D.
at the middle of His public life 29 A.D.
and at the end 30 A.D.

FIRST PASSOVER

March 28 A.D. When Jesus cleanses temple, Jews said it was 46 years in the building (John 2:19). Herod began rebuilding the temple around 20-19 B.C. Therefore the first Passover in Jesus' public ministry was that of 28 A.D.

April 28 Jesus talks with Nicodemus
The Baptist's last witness concerning Jesus

May 28	John is arrested
	Jesus returns to Galilee by way of Samaria:
	encounter the Samaritan woman at Jacob's well
	Preaches and cures in Galilee
	Calls Peter, Andrew, James and John
June 28	Cures at Capernaum and environs
	5 conflicts with Scribes and Pharisees
	The call of Matthew
	The call of the Twelve
July 28	Sermon on the Mount
Aug -Sep 28	Preaching, cures centurion's servant
	raises son of widow of Naim
	gives witness concerning John the Baptist
	feet anointed by Mary Magdalene
	Holy women administer to Jesus and apostles
	Lk.8:1-3
Oct. 28	Jesus teaches in parables (four deal with sowing
	of the crops; therefore, Oct. or Nov.)
Nov-Dec 28	Jesus calms storm
	exorcises possessed in land of the Gerasene
	cures woman of Hemorrhage
	raises daughter of Jairus
	rejected at Nazareth
	first missionary journey of the twelve.
Jan-Feb 29	execution of John the Baptist
	[John came out of the desert Oct. 27 A.D.
	was imprisoned May 28 A.D.
	was eulogized by Jesus Sept. 28 A.D.
	was executed by Herod in springtime of 29]

SECOND PASSOVER

Mar.-Apr. 29   First multiplication of loaves on northeastern shore of the Lake of Galilee about three miles from where the Jordan enters the Lake, in a desert place near Bethsaida Julias (a town beautified by Philip and named by him Julias in honor of Augustus' daughter, Julia).
Discourse on bread of life

May-July29   After the discourse on bread of life, Jesus temporarily lost the popular support that had sustained him against the intrigues of the Scribes and Pharisees. So He departed for lands to the north and east of Galilee: Tyre and Sidon on the Mediterranean coast and the Greek cities of the Decapolis beyond the Jordan and to the slopes of Mt. Hermon where the Jordan arose (Carroll p. 337)

    This was the first time since the flight into Egypt, that Jesus went beyond the boundaries of the Promised Land.

June 29   In the district of Tyre and Sidon, Jesus cures daughter of the Canaanite woman. She was the second pagan for whom Jesus worked a miracle. The first was the centurion. Both were noted for their faith.

July 29   In the district of Decapolis, east and southeast of the Lake of Galilee, He multiplies loaves a second time then He crosses the lake and confronts the Scribes and Pharisees at Dalmanutha on the western shore of the lake from there He heads north to Bethsaida Julias and cures a blind man going farther north to Caearea-Philippi, Peter confesses to Jesus to be the Son of God; Jesus in turn promises that Peter will be head of His Church. leaving Caesarea-Philippi, Jesus heads south on the eastern side of the Lake of Galilee, makes His first prediction of His passion and resurrection, crossed the Jordan for Mt. Tabor.

August 29   Transfiguration on Mt. Tabor. heads for Capernaum; second prediction of His passion and resurrection' final teachings in Galilee

September 29 Jesus leaves Galilee
mission of the 72 disciples (some put this after the Feast of Tabernacles, but this seems hardly possible in view of the hostility raised against Jesus at this feast)

October 29   The Feast of Tabernacles was one of the three greatest feasts in the Jewish religious year (the other two were Passover and Pentecost)

In the year 29, the Feast probably started on Oct. 15.

When the feast was half over (Oct 18th or 19th), Jesus went to the temple to preach.

Jesus proclaimed Himself as the fulfillment of the very symbolism of this feast.

The Feast was marked by three solemn ceremonies:

1.   Libations: each day of the Feast, at the morning sacrifice, water was brought in a golden vessel from the pool of Siloam in solemn procession to the temple where, with music and song, it was poured out as a libation on the altar.

It commemorated the water springing miraculously from the rock in the desert at the touch of Moses' rod.

John chap. 7: Jesus proclaims Himself the rock from whom will flow rivers of living water.

2.   Tents: the Law of Moses prescribed that for eight days of the Feast, each family was to dwell

in tents (tabernacle) to commemorate the forty years Israel dwelt in tents in the desert after leaving Egypt.

John chap. 8: a spirit of Mardi Gras was abroad at this time; hence the woman taken in adultery.

3. Lights: each evening of the Feast, the court of the women was lit up by great branching candelabra, 150 feet high, illuminating the city as though it were day.

This occasioned Jesus' remark: "I am the light of the world."

John ch. 9: then to prove He was the light of the world, Jesus gave the light of sight to a man born blind by having him wash in the pool of Siloam.

4. Life: Jesus proclaims He is the good shepherd.

John ch. 10: Jesus is the new Moses, leading his sheep to the promised land of eternal life.

November 29 Jesus in Judea
teaching on prayer

December 29 The Feast of the Dedication (December 22, 29 A.D.)

This Feast was instituted by Judas Maccabeus in 164 B.C. to remove the desecration of the temple by Antiochus Epiphanes. It was called the Feast of Lights (Hanukkah), because the temple was brilliantly illuminated on the first and last days of the feast.

On this Feast Jesus again claimed to be one with the Father. The Jews tried to stone Him. He fled to the district of Judea beyond the Jordan, to Perea.

Jan-Feb 30   Jesus' teachings in Perea
parables of lost sheep, lost coin, lost son
four lessons on the use of wealth

March 30   teaching on marriage and divorce
while teaching in Perea, Martha and Mary send
Jesus a message about Lazarus being sick.
raising of Lazarus
Sanhedrin conspires to kill Jesus
Jesus flees to Ephrem, 17 miles northeast of Jerusalem. The Passover of 30 A.D. was near.
Jesus left Ephrem for Jerusalem by way of Jericho. On the way He makes the third prediction of His passion and resurrection.
at Jericho He converts Zaccheus. Leaving Jericho.
He cures the blind man Bartimaeus. Then He went to Bethany. It was March 31, 30 A.D.
Jesus stayed two nights at the home of Martha and Mary.
On the second night, at the home of Simon the Leper, Mary anointed the feet of Jesus. It was April 1, 30 A.D.

THIRD PASSOVER

April 30   On Sun. April 2, Jesus entered Jerusalem—
Palm Sunday. That night and on Monday and Tuesday, He stayed at the home of Martha and Mary.
Mon. April 4, denounces Pharisees
Wed. April 5, Judas offers to betray Jesus
Thurs. April 6, Last Supper, Agony in Garden
Fri. April 7, Crucifixion
That evening Passover began
Sat. April 8, Jesus in the tomb
Sun. April 9, Resurrection

May 5, 30 A.D.   The Ascension of Jesus into heaven (Acts 1)

May 29, 30 A.D. Pentecost (Acts 2)

30-37 A.D.   Peter heads the Church in Jerusalem (Act 3-6)

Dec. 36 A.D.   Pontius Pilate removed from office

Spring 37 A.D.   Conversion of Saul on the road to Damascus (Acts 9)

39 A.D.   Saul returns to Jerusalem

40 A.D.   Conversion of Cornelius (Acts 10-11)

40-41   Herod Agrippa becomes king of Judea

Jul. 14, 42 A.D. Dispersion of the apostles:
Andrew to Scythia and perhaps Greece
Bartholomew to south Arabia, perhaps India
Jude Thaddeus to Syria
Matthew to Armenia and/or Ethiopia
Matthias entirely unknown
Philip to Asia Minor
Simon Zealotes to Mesopotamia
Thomas to Parthia and India

41-42 A.D.   **St. Matthew wrote his gospel in Aramaic for the faithful in Judea and in Greek for the Jews of the Dispersion.** He did this with the help of the other apostles before they dispersed beyond the boundaries of the Roman empire, to teach all nations as Jesus had commanded them.

Also John probably took Mary to Ephesus at this time and stayed there till the death of Agrippa in 44 A.D.

42 A.D.   Martyrdom of St. James, brother of John
Peter imprisoned in Jerusalem, escapes and departs thence for his first sojourn in Rome from 42 to 49 A.D.

44 A.D.   Herod Agrippa dies

45-49 A.D.   Paul's first Missionary Journey (Acts 13-14)

49 A.D.   Expulsion of all Jews from Rome by Claudius
Tradition says Mary died in Jerusalem in 49 A.D. at the age of 69, on the eve of the Council of Jerusalem, that was why the apostles happened to be in Jerusalem for the Council.

50 A.D.   Council of Jerusalem (Acts 15)

50-53 A.D.   Paul's Second Missionary Journey (Acts 15-18)
1 and 2 Thessalonians written

50 -54 A.D.   Peter leaves the Council for Antioch, Bithynia and Cappadocia

54-57 A.D.   Claudia dies, so Peter returns to Rome—his second sojourn there
Gospel of Mark written under Peter's direction

54-58 A.D.   Paul's Third Missionary Journey (Act 18-21)
1 and 2 Corinthians, Galatians, Romans written

57-62 A.D.   Peter leaves Rome to strengthen the Church in Bithynia, Pontus and Cappadocia
Mark goes to Alexandria and founds the church there

58 A.D.   Paul's imprisonment at Jerusalem (Acts 27-28)

58-60 A.D.	Paul imprisoned in Caesarea (Acts 23-26) **Luke writes his gospel**
60-61 A.D.	Paul's journey to Rome (Act 27-28)
61-63 A.D.	Paul in chains in Rome (Acts 28) **Ephesians, Philippians, Colossions, Philemon** **Luke writes Acts of Apostles**
62-67 A.D.	Peter's third and last sojourn in Rome **1 and 2 Peter written** Mark returns from Alexandria to be with Peter
67 A.D.	Peter martyred on Vatican Hill Paul martyred outside the walls of Rome
68 A.D.	Mark returns to Alexandria and is martyred
90 A.D.	**The Gospel according to John**
96 A.D.	**The Book of Revelation**